Samsung Galaxy S25 Ultra

Ultra

Camera User Manual

Master Every Shot: A Complete Guide with
illustration to Unlocking Creative Potential and
Capturing Stunning Moments with Advanced
Photography Features | For Beginners & Advanced
User's

Miles Techton

Miles Techton

Table of Contents

SAMSUNG
Galaxy S25 Ultra
Guad-Canepry

Night Mode

Night Mode

Editing Tools

Nighlrt Mode

Editing Tools

Introduction: Why the Galaxy S25 Ultra is a Game-Changer

The Samsung Galaxy S25 Ultra redefines smartphone photography, setting a new benchmark for both casual users and photography enthusiasts. With cutting-edge hardware and intelligent software, this flagship device offers unparalleled versatility, making it an essential tool for capturing life's moments with precision and creativity.

Exclusive Features Overview

Revolutionary Camera Hardware

The Galaxy S25 Ultra boasts a **quad-camera system** that delivers professional-grade results:

- **200MP Primary Sensor**: Building on its predecessor's success, the 200MP sensor ensures stunning detail and clarity, even in challenging lighting conditions.

- **50MP Ultrawide Lens**: A significant upgrade from the previous 12MP sensor, this lens captures expansive landscapes and group shots with exceptional sharpness. Autofocus capabilities make it perfect for macro photography as well.

- **50MP Telephoto Lens (3x Optical Zoom)**: Enhanced with Optical Image Stabilization (OIS), this lens provides crisp, stable zoomed-in shots, ideal for portraits and mid-range photography.

- **50MP Super-Telephoto Lens (5x Optical Zoom)**: Perfect for distant subjects, this lens combines high resolution with advanced zoom capabilities for breathtaking detail.

These upgrades represent a leap forward in mobile imaging, ensuring that every shot — whether wide-angle or zoomed in — is rich in detail and vibrancy.

AI-Powered Enhancements

Samsung has integrated advanced AI features to simplify photography while delivering professional results:

- **Scene Optimization**: Automatically adjusts settings like exposure, color balance, and focus based on the subject and environment.

- **Object Eraser**: Effortlessly removes unwanted elements from photos with a single tap, ensuring clean and polished images.

- **Low-Light Mastery**: AI algorithms enhance night photography by reducing noise and optimizing dynamic range, making it easier to capture stunning shots in dim conditions.

Versatility for Every User

Whether you're an aspiring photographer or a casual user snapping everyday moments, the Galaxy S25 Ultra adapts to your needs:

- **Casual Users**: The intuitive camera app and AI-driven features make it easy to capture great photos without technical expertise.

- **Photography Enthusiasts**: Advanced tools like Pro Mode and RAW capture provide creative control over every aspect of your shots.

How This Guide Will Transform Your Photography: What to Expect

Whether you're a beginner just starting out or an experienced photographer looking to push creative boundaries, this guide is designed to elevate your photography skills step by step.

What You'll Learn in This Guide

1. **Mastering the Basics**

   - Get started with the camera setup, understanding its interface, and configuring essential settings.

   - Learn how to use AI-powered features like **Scene Optimization** for automatic adjustments and **Object Eraser** for quick photo clean-up.

2. **Exploring Advanced Camera Features**

   - Dive into **Pro Mode** to take full control of settings like ISO, shutter speed, and focus.

   - Understand the benefits of shooting in **RAW format** for professional-grade editing.

   - Discover how to utilize the upgraded **50MP ultrawide lens** and dual telephoto lenses (3x and 5x) for versatile photography styles.

3. **Photography Techniques for Every Scenario**

- Capture stunning portraits with the enhanced 3x telephoto lens and its improved low-light performance.

- Perfect your landscape shots using the 50MP ultrawide lens with pixel-binning technology for sharper details.

- Experiment with macro photography and hybrid zoom for intricate close-ups and distant subjects.

4. **Low-Light Mastery**

   - Learn how to make the most of the 200MP sensor and AI algorithms to capture breathtaking night shots.

   - Explore techniques like long exposure photography for creative effects.

5. **Video Recording Excellence**

   - Unlock the potential of 8K video recording with tips on stabilization, framing, and editing.

   - Use features like Audio Eraser to remove background noise from your videos.

6. **Editing Like a Pro**

   - Step-by-step guidance on editing photos directly on your phone using built-in tools or third-party apps.

   - Tips for enhancing colors, cropping, and retouching images for a polished final result.

How This Guide Will Help You

- **Step-by-Step Instructions:** Each feature is broken down into simple, actionable steps with accompanying screenshots or diagrams.

- **Real-World Scenarios:** Practical examples tailored to everyday situations—whether you're capturing travel memories, food photography, or family portraits.

- **Expert Tips:** Gain insights from photography professionals on composition, lighting, and creative techniques.

- **Interactive Challenges:** Engage in quizzes and photo challenges to test your skills and inspire experimentation.

Let's get started on transforming your photography!

Chapter 1: Getting Started with the Galaxy S25 Ultra Camera

The Samsung Galaxy S25 Ultra camera is designed to deliver professional-grade results right out of the box. This chapter will guide you through the unboxing and initial setup process, ensuring you're ready to explore its powerful features.

Unboxing and Initial Setup: Step-by-Step Guide

What's Included in the Box

USB-C Cable

SIM Ejector Tool

When you unbox your Galaxy S25 Ultra, you'll find:

- **Samsung Galaxy S25 Ultra** (available in colors like Icy Blue, Phantom Black, and Cream).

- **USB-C Cable** for charging and data transfer.

- **SIM Ejector Tool** to insert your SIM card.

- **Quick Start Guide** with basic instructions.

- **Warranty Card** for product support.

Note: Samsung has discontinued including a charging brick in the box, so you'll need to purchase one separately if required.

Step-by-Step Setup Instructions

1. **Unboxing Your Device**

   o   Carefully remove the Galaxy S25 Ultra from its box.

   o   Inspect the device for any damage and ensure all accessories are included.

2. **Powering On**

   o   Press and hold the **Power Button** (located on the right side) until the Samsung logo appears.

   o   Follow the on-screen prompts to select your language and region.

3. **Connecting to Wi-Fi**

   o   Choose a Wi-Fi network during setup or use mobile data for initial updates.

   o   Enter your password and wait for confirmation.

4. **Installing Updates**

   o   Once connected, your phone will check for software updates. Install any available updates to ensure optimal performance and access to the latest camera features.

5. **Configuring AI Features**

   o Navigate to **Settings > Camera > AI Enhancements**.

   o Enable options like:

     ▪ **Scene Optimization**: Automatically adjusts settings based on your subject.

     ▪ **Object Eraser**: Allows easy removal of unwanted elements from photos.

6. **Setting Up Pro Mode**

   o Open the camera app and swipe to "Pro Mode."

   o Familiarize yourself with manual controls like ISO, shutter speed, and white balance.

7. **Exploring Camera Lenses**

   o Test each lens by switching between modes:

     ▪ Ultrawide (50MP) for landscapes.

     ▪ Telephoto (3x and 5x zoom) for portraits or distant subjects.

     ▪ Primary sensor (200MP) for high-resolution shots.

Navigating the Camera Interface Like a Pro: Screenshots and Tips

The Galaxy S25 Ultra camera interface is designed to be intuitive yet powerful, offering a seamless experience for both casual users and photography enthusiasts. This section will guide you through the layout of the camera app, highlight its key features, and provide tips for customizing the interface to suit your needs.

Understanding the Camera Interface Layout

When you open the camera app, you'll see a clean and organized interface with all essential tools easily accessible. Here's a breakdown of the main elements:

1. **Mode Selector (Bottom Bar):**

   o Swipe left or right to switch between modes such as **Photo**, **Video**, **Portrait**, **Pro Mode**, and more.

   o Tap "More" to access additional modes like Night, Panorama, Super Slow-Mo, and Food.

2. **Shutter Button (Center):**

   o The large circular button in the middle is used to capture photos or start/stop recording videos.

3. **Zoom Controls (Right Side):**

- Use the zoom slider to switch between lenses:
  - 0.6x for ultrawide shots.
  - 1x for standard photos.
  - 3x and 5x for telephoto zoom.

4. **Settings Menu (Top Left)**:

   - Access advanced settings by tapping the gear icon. Here, you can enable features like grid lines, HDR, and RAW capture.

5. **AI Features (Top Center)**:

   - Toggle Scene Optimization or Object Eraser directly from the top bar.

6. **Gallery Shortcut (Bottom Left)**:

   - Quickly preview your last photo or video by tapping the thumbnail.

7. **Customizable Toolbar (Top Right)**:

   - Add shortcuts for frequently used tools like Flash, Filters, or Aspect Ratio adjustments.

Tips for Customizing the Interface

1. **Add Favorite Modes to Quick Access**:

   - Long-press any mode in the "More" section and drag it to the bottom bar for quicker access.

2. **Enable Grid Lines**:

- o Go to Settings > Camera > Grid Lines to enable a rule-of-thirds overlay for better composition.

3. **Adjust Shutter Sound**:

- o In Settings, toggle off the shutter sound if you prefer silent shooting.

4. **Customize Pro Mode Toolbar**:

- o In Pro Mode settings, rearrange controls like ISO, white balance, and focus to match your workflow.

Annotated Screenshot Example

Screenshot Layout

Element	Description
Mode Selector	Swipeable bar at the bottom of the screen.
Shutter Button	Large circular button in the center.
Zoom Slider	Adjustable zoom levels on the right side.
Settings Icon	Gear icon in the top-left corner.
AI Features Toggle	Scene Optimization toggle at top-center.
Gallery Shortcut	Thumbnail preview at bottom-left corner.

Pro Tips for Efficient Navigation

❖ **Quick Zoom Switching**: Double-tap on the zoom slider to instantly switch between 1x, 3x, and 5x zoom levels without dragging.

❖ **One-Handed Operation**: Enable one-handed mode in system settings if you find it difficult to reach all controls on the large screen.

To enable **One-Handed Operation** on your Samsung Galaxy S25 Ultra, follow these steps:

1. **Open Settings**:
   - Locate and tap the **Settings** app on your home screen or in the app drawer.
2. **Navigate to Advanced Features**:
   - Scroll down and select **Advanced Features**.
3. **Enable One-Handed Mode**:
   - Tap on **One-handed mode**.
   - Toggle the switch at the top of the screen to enable this feature.
4. **Choose Activation Method**:
   - Select your preferred method to activate One-Handed Mode:
     - **Gesture**: Swipe down in the center of the bottom edge of the screen.
     - **Button**: Double-tap the Home button (if using button navigation).
5. **Adjust Panel Position**:
   - Tap the arrow on the side of the minimized screen to move it to either side based on your preference.

6. **Exit One-Handed Mode**:
   - ○ Tap on the empty space outside the minimized window or use your chosen activation method again.

This feature is particularly useful for users with larger devices, as it makes navigation easier by reducing the screen size and positioning it within reach of your thumb.

- ❖ **Save Custom Presets in Pro Mode**: After adjusting settings like ISO or shutter speed in Pro Mode, save them as a preset for quick reuse during similar shoots.

Quick Start Guide for Beginners: Essential Settings to Adjust Before You Start

Essential Settings for Beginners

1. Select the Right Resolution

The Galaxy S25 Ultra offers three resolution options:

- **12MP**: Ideal for everyday photography and social media sharing. Provides a balance between quality and file size.

- **50MP**: Perfect for capturing intricate textures and details without consuming excessive storage.

- **200MP**: Best for ultra-high-resolution photography, capturing exceptional clarity. Note that zoom functionality is disabled in this mode, so careful composition is required.

To adjust:

- Open the **Camera app** > Tap the **Settings icon** > Select **Resolution** > Choose your preferred option.

2. Adjust Aspect Ratio

Choose an aspect ratio that fits your needs:

- **16:9**: Great for widescreen shots or videos.
- **1:1**: Perfect for Instagram posts.
- **Full Screen**: Utilizes the entire display for immersive photography.

To set:

- In the Camera app, tap the **Quick controls (four dots)** > Select **Ratio** > Pick your desired aspect ratio.

3. Enable Stabilization for Videos

For smooth video recording:

- Turn on **Super Steady Stabilization**, which minimizes motion blur during handheld or action-packed filming.
- Navigate to Camera settings > Video mode > Enable **Super Steady Stabilization**.

4. Activate Scene Optimizer

The Scene Optimizer uses AI to adjust settings like exposure, contrast, and white balance based on the subject and environment. This feature is especially helpful for beginners who want automatic enhancements.

- Go to **Settings** > Enable **Scene Optimizer** under Intelligent Features.

5. Enable AI Enhancements

Activate features like:

- **Shot Suggestions**: Provides on-screen guides for better composition.
- **Object Eraser**: Removes unwanted elements from photos with a single tap.

To enable:

- Open Settings > Navigate to Intelligent Features > Toggle these options on.

Troubleshooting Common Setup Issues

1. **Camera App Not Launching**

   o Ensure your phone is updated to the latest software version.

   o Restart your device if the app freezes.

2. **Scene Optimizer Not Working**

   o Check that it's enabled in settings under Intelligent Features.

   o Ensure you're using the rear camera, as Scene Optimizer is unavailable on the front camera.

3. **Blurry Photos**

   o Clean the camera lens with a microfiber cloth.

   o Use tracking autofocus to keep moving subjects sharp.

Next Steps

Once these settings are adjusted, you're ready to start exploring the Galaxy S25 Ultra's features.

Chapter 2: Unlocking the Camera Hardware Potential

The Samsung Galaxy S25 Ultra is equipped with a state-of-the-art camera system that pushes the boundaries of mobile photography. This chapter provides a comprehensive breakdown of its lenses, their specific uses, and how to maximize their potential for stunning results.

Comprehensive Breakdown of Camera Lenses

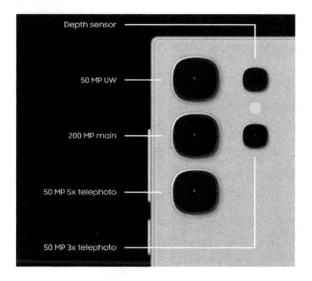

1. 200MP Primary Sensor
- **Specifications**: The flagship 200MP sensor offers unmatched clarity and detail, making it ideal for capturing high-resolution images. It uses advanced pixel-binning technology to combine smaller pixels into larger ones for enhanced low-light performance.
- **Best Uses**:

- o **Portraits**: Achieve sharp details and vibrant colors.
- o **Landscape Photography**: Capture expansive views with incredible depth and detail.
- o **Low-Light Shots**: Pixel-binning ensures bright and noise-free images in dim conditions.
- **Example**: A cityscape at sunset, showcasing intricate building details and vibrant hues.

2. 50MP Ultrawide Lens (UW)

- **Specifications**: The ultrawide lens features a 1/2.52-inch optical format, 0.7µm pixel size, and an F1.9 aperture. It includes autofocus capabilities, making it versatile for both wide-angle shots and macro photography.
- **Best Uses**:
  - o **Landscapes**: Perfect for capturing sweeping vistas or group photos.
  - o **Macro Photography**: Autofocus allows close-up shots of intricate textures like flowers or insects.
  - o **Video Recording**: Supports 4K at 60fps or 8K at 30fps for immersive wide-angle videos.
- **Example**: A breathtaking mountain range or a close-up of a flower revealing fine details.

3. Telephoto Lenses (3x and 5x Optical Zoom)

- **Specifications**:
  - o **3x Telephoto Lens**: Features Optical Image Stabilization (OIS) for sharper mid-range zoom shots, ideal for portraits.
  - o **5x Telephoto Lens**: Offers higher zoom levels with OIS, perfect for distant subjects.
- **Best Uses**:

- o **Portraits**: Create beautiful bokeh effects with precise subject focus.
- o **Wildlife Photography**: Capture animals from a distance without disturbing them.
- o **Event Photography**: Zoom in on key moments while maintaining image quality.
- **Example**:
  - o A close-up shot of a bird perched on a tree using the 5x zoom lens.

Lens Type	Position on Device
Primary Sensor	Centered at the top of the camera module
Ultrawide Lens	Positioned at the top of the primary sensor
Telephoto (3x Zoom)	Adjacent to the ultrawide lens
Telephoto (5x Zoom)	Below the Primary Sensor

Tips for Maximizing Hardware Potential

1. **Switch Between Lenses Seamlessly**

   - o Use the zoom slider to transition between ultrawide, standard, and telephoto lenses effortlessly.
2. **Leverage Autofocus in Ultrawide Mode**
   - o Experiment with macro shots by moving closer to your subject while maintaining sharp focus.
3. **Enable Optical Image Stabilization**
   - o For telephoto shots, ensure OIS is active in settings to avoid blurry images.

4. **Use Pro Mode for Manual Adjustments**
   - Adjust ISO, shutter speed, and white balance to tailor each lens's performance to your needs.

Revolutionary Sensor Technology and Image Processing Power: How It Enhances Photos

The Samsung Galaxy S25 Ultra introduces groundbreaking advancements in sensor technology and image processing, setting a new standard for mobile photography. With enhanced hardware and smarter algorithms, this device ensures sharper, brighter, and more detailed images across all scenarios.

Sensor Improvements: Pixel-Binning Technology and Larger Sensors

Pixel-Binning Technology

- The Galaxy S25 Ultra employs **pixel-binning** in its sensors, particularly the 200MP primary sensor. This technique combines multiple smaller pixels into one larger "super-pixel," significantly improving light absorption and reducing noise in low-light conditions.

- The ultrawide lens also benefits from pixel-binning, upgrading from the 12MP sensor in the Galaxy S24 Ultra to a **50MP ISOCELL JN1 sensor**, which enhances image resolution and detail.

Larger Sensors for Better Light Absorption

- The 3x telephoto camera has been upgraded to a **1/3-inch ISOCELL sensor**, larger than the 1/3.52-inch sensor in the Galaxy S24 Ultra. This increase in size improves light absorption, resulting in brighter and sharper zoomed-in shots.

- Larger sensors allow for better dynamic range, capturing more detail in shadows and highlights, especially in challenging lighting conditions.

Comparisons Between Galaxy S24 Ultra and S25 Ultra Hardware

Feature	Galaxy S24 Ultra	Galaxy S25 Ultra	Improvement
Primary Sensor	200MP	200MP	Same sensor size but improved algorithms.
Ultrawide Sensor	12MP (1/2.55-inch)	50MP (1/2.76-inch ISOCELL JN1)	Higher resolution for sharper images.
3x Telephoto Sensor	10MP (1/3.52-inch)	50MP (1/3-inch ISOCELL)	Larger sensor for better zoom quality.
5x Telephoto Sensor	50MP	50MP	No change; retains excellent zoom capabilities.

The jump in resolution and sensor size for the ultrawide and telephoto cameras marks a significant leap forward, offering sharper details and improved performance compared to the Galaxy S24 Ultra.

Enhanced Image Processing Power

Samsung has paired these hardware upgrades with advanced AI-driven algorithms:

- **Improved Scene Optimization**: Automatically adjusts exposure, focus, and color balance based on the subject.

- **New Image Processing Algorithms**: These enhance photo clarity and reduce artifacts, particularly in high-resolution shots or zoomed images.

- **Low-Light Performance**: Combined with larger sensors, AI algorithms further reduce noise while boosting brightness and detail in dim environments.

Real-World Impact on Photography

These advancements translate into noticeable improvements across various photography styles:

- **Portraits**: Achieve stunning bokeh effects with sharper subject focus using the upgraded telephoto lenses.

- **Landscapes**: Capture expansive vistas with higher resolution ultrawide shots.

- **Night Photography**: Pixel-binning technology ensures vibrant shots even in near-darkness.

- **Zoomed Shots**: Enhanced telephoto sensors deliver crisp details at both 3x and 5x optical zoom levels.

The Samsung Galaxy S25 Ultra's revolutionary sensor technology and smarter image processing empower users to capture professional-grade photos effortlessly. Whether you're shooting portraits, landscapes, or low-light scenes, this device ensures every shot is exceptional.

AI Enhancements: What Sets the Galaxy S25 Ultra Apart from Competitors

The Samsung Galaxy S25 Ultra leverages cutting-edge AI-powered features to elevate mobile photography and editing efficiency, distinguishing itself from competitors like Apple and OnePlus. With tools such as Scene Optimization, Object Eraser, and Live Focus, the device simplifies complex tasks while delivering professional-grade results.

Key AI Features

1. Scene Optimization

- **What It Does**: Automatically adjusts settings like exposure, white balance, and focus based on the subject and environment. For example, it identifies whether you're shooting a landscape, portrait, or food photo and tailors the camera settings accordingly.
- **How It Improves Composition**:
    - Ensures balanced lighting and vibrant colors without manual intervention.
    - Reduces overexposure in bright conditions and enhances shadows in dim environments.
- **Real-Life Example**: Capturing a sunset over the ocean— Scene Optimization adjusts to preserve the warm tones of the sky while enhancing the texture of waves.

2. Object Eraser

- **What It Does**: Removes unwanted elements from photos with a single tap, using AI to seamlessly fill in the background.
- **How It Improves Editing Efficiency**:
  - Saves time compared to manual editing in third-party apps.
  - Maintains natural-looking results by analyzing surrounding pixels.
- **Real-Life Example**: Removing a photobomber from a group photo at a crowded event, leaving the background intact.

3. Live Focus

- **What It Does**: Uses AI to apply depth-of-field effects for professional-looking portraits. It allows users to adjust blur intensity even after capturing the photo.
- **How It Enhances Composition**:
  - Highlights subjects by creating a soft bokeh effect in the background.
  - Adds creative flair to portraits and close-ups.
- **Real-Life Example**: Capturing a close-up of a flower with blurred foliage in the background, emphasizing the subject.

Why It Stands Out

1. **Efficiency vs Competitors**:
   - Unlike OnePlus's AI zoom enhancements or Apple's computational photography features, Samsung's tools integrate seamlessly into the user experience

without requiring additional apps or manual adjustments.

- o Features like Object Eraser are intuitive and faster than similar tools on other platforms.

2. **Real-Time AI Integration**:

- o Samsung's AI works dynamically during both capture and post-processing stages, ensuring high-quality results without extensive user input.

3. **Enhanced Versatility**:

- o These features cater to both casual users who want automatic improvements and professionals seeking creative control via tools like Expert RAW.

Real-Life Scenarios Illustrating AI Enhancements

1. **Travel Photography**:

- o Scene Optimization adjusts for varying light conditions when photographing landmarks like the Golden Gate Bridge at sunset.

- o Object Eraser removes distractions such as tourists from your shot effortlessly.

2. **Event Photography**:

- o Live Focus creates stunning portraits during weddings or parties by isolating subjects against blurred backgrounds.

3. **Night Photography**:

o   AI algorithms reduce noise and enhance brightness when capturing cityscapes under low-light conditions.

Samsung's Galaxy S25 Ultra sets itself apart with intuitive AI-powered tools that simplify complex tasks while delivering exceptional results. Whether you're capturing everyday moments or crafting artistic masterpieces, these features ensure every shot is polished and professional.

Chapter 3: Photography Fundamentals – Mastering Everyday Shots

Lighting Basics for Stunning Photos: Natural Light vs. Artificial Light

Lighting is the cornerstone of photography—it shapes the mood, tone, and quality of your images. Whether you're shooting outdoors under the sun or indoors with artificial light, understanding how to harness these light sources effectively will transform your everyday shots. This section explores the differences between natural and artificial light and provides actionable tips for mastering both.

How Lighting Affects Photo Quality

1. **Natural Light**:

- **Golden Hour**: The soft, warm light during sunrise and sunset creates flattering tones and gentle shadows, ideal for portraits and landscapes.

- **Harsh Midday Light**: Direct sunlight from above can create strong shadows and overexposed highlights. Using reflectors or diffusers can help soften these effects.

2. **Artificial Light**:

- Offers complete control over intensity, direction, and color temperature. It's perfect for creating specific moods or replicating consistent lighting conditions indoors.

- Techniques like **three-point lighting** (key light, fill light, backlight) ensure balanced illumination and subject separation from the background.

Using Natural Light Effectively

Outdoors

- **Golden Hour Advantage**:

  - Shoot during early morning or late afternoon for soft, diffused light that enhances colors and reduces harsh shadows.

  - Example: A portrait taken at sunset with warm tones bathing the subject.

- **Overcast Conditions**:

- Clouds act as natural diffusers, creating soft light that minimizes contrast. Ideal for even lighting in portraits or product photography.
- Example: A close-up of a flower on a cloudy day with subtle shadows.

Indoors

- Position subjects near windows to utilize filtered sunlight. For softer effects, use sheer curtains to diffuse the light further.
- Example: A cozy indoor portrait with natural light streaming through a window.

Using Artificial Light Effectively

Studio Lighting

- Use LED panels or strobes to control brightness and direction.
- Diffuse harsh artificial light with softboxes or umbrellas for a balanced look.

Creative Applications

- Experiment with rim lighting (backlight at an angle) to create glowing outlines around your subject for dramatic effects.
- Example: A silhouette of a dancer with rim lighting highlighting their form.

Three-Point Lighting Setup

- **Key Light**: Main source of illumination.

- **Fill Light**: Reduces shadows created by the key light.

- **Backlight**: Separates the subject from the background for depth.

Comparing Natural vs. Artificial Lighting Effects

Feature	Natural Light	Artificial Light
Control	Limited; depends on time/weather	Complete control over intensity/direction
Cost	Free	Requires investment in equipment
Mood Creation	Warm tones during golden hour	Wide range of moods (dramatic or soft)
Convenience	Ideal for outdoor shoots	Best for night or indoor photography

Real-Life Examples

1. **Natural Light Portrait**:

    o   Taken at golden hour outdoors, showcasing warm tones and flattering shadows.

    o   Mood: Romantic and serene.

2. **Artificial Light Product Shot**:

    o   Studio setup with diffused LED panels creating even lighting on a product.

    o   Mood: Professional and polished.

Autofocus vs. Manual Focus Techniques: When to Use Each

Both autofocus (AF) and manual focus (MF) are essential tools for photographers, each excelling in specific scenarios. Understanding when and how to use them can significantly improve your ability to capture sharp, well-composed images.

Autofocus: When It Excels

Autofocus is the default mode for most photographers due to its speed, accuracy, and ease of use. Galaxy S25 Ultra, other smartphones and Modern cameras, offer advanced autofocus modes tailored to different situations:

Scenarios Where Autofocus Shines

1. **Moving Subjects**:

    o   Use **AF-C (Continuous AF)** for tracking fast-moving subjects like athletes or wildlife. The camera continuously adjusts focus as the subject moves within the frame.

- o Example: Capturing a runner in motion with sharp focus on their face.

2. **Portraits**:

- o Autofocus ensures precise focus on the subject's eyes, especially with AI enhancements like eye-tracking.

o   Example: A close-up portrait with perfect focus on the eyes while maintaining a blurred background.

3. **Low-Light Conditions**:

o   Autofocus algorithms can detect contrast differences even in dim environments, ensuring clear shots without manual adjustments.

o   Example: Night photography of cityscapes or indoor events.

Manual Focus: When It's Essential

Manual focus provides complete control over the focus point, making it ideal for situations where autofocus struggles or when precision is paramount.

Scenarios Where Manual Focus Excels

1. **Macro Photography**:

o   Autofocus may struggle to lock onto tiny details at close distances. Manual focus allows you to precisely target small areas like water droplets or flower petals.

o   Example: A macro shot of a dew-covered leaf with sharp focus on a single droplet.

2. **Landscape Photography**:

o   For static scenes, manual focus ensures pinpoint accuracy on distant subjects without relying on autofocus algorithms.

o   Example: Focusing on a mountain range during sunrise for maximum sharpness across the frame.

3. **Astrophotography**:

o   Autofocus often fails in low-light conditions with minimal contrast, making manual focus essential for capturing stars or the Milky Way.

o   Example: A starry night sky with sharp stars and no blurring.

How to Switch Between Focus Modes on the Galaxy S25 Ultra

Step-by-Step Instructions

1. **Access Camera Settings**:

o   Open the camera app and tap the settings icon in the top-left corner.

2. **Select Focus Mode**:

o   Navigate to "Focus Mode" and choose between **Autofocus (AF)** and **Manual Focus (MF)**.

3. **Adjust Manual Focus**:

o   In MF mode, use the on-screen slider or touch controls to fine-tune focus until your subject appears sharp.

4. **Use MF Assist Features**:

o   Enable tools like Focus Peaking (highlights areas in focus) or Magnifier for precise adjustments.

Illustration Demonstrating Focus Differences

Scenario	Autofocus Example	Manual Focus Example
Moving Subject	Bird in flight captured sharply	Blurred motion due to MF adjustments
Macro Photography	Struggles to lock onto tiny details	Sharp droplet-focused macro shot
Landscape Photography	AI-selected focal point may miss details	Crisp mountain range using MF

Tips for Choosing Between Autofocus and Manual Focus

- Use autofocus for dynamic scenes like moving subjects or portraits where speed is crucial.

- Switch to manual focus for static subjects requiring precision or challenging conditions like extreme close-ups or astrophotography.

HDR and Scene Optimization Simplified: Real-Life Examples

The Samsung Galaxy S25 Ultra is equipped with advanced HDR (High Dynamic Range) and AI-powered Scene Optimization features, making it easier than ever to capture stunning photos. These tools help balance brightness, contrast, and color, ensuring your images look vibrant and professional in a variety of lighting conditions. Let's explore how they work and when to use them, with real-life examples.

Understanding HDR: High Dynamic Range

What is HDR?

HDR enhances photos by balancing the extremes of light and shadow in high-contrast scenes. It combines multiple exposures of the same shot — bright, medium, and dark — to create a single image with improved detail in both highlights and shadows.

When to Use HDR

1. **High-Contrast Scenes**:
   - Ideal for situations where parts of the image are overly bright while others are too dark.
   - Example: A sunset photo where the sky is bright but foreground objects are in shadow.
2. **Landscape Photography**:
   - Captures details in both the bright sky and darker ground elements.
   - Example: A mountain range with sunlight streaming through clouds.
3. **Indoor Scenes with Backlighting**:
   - Balances light from windows with darker indoor areas.
   - Example: A portrait taken indoors with sunlight streaming through a window.

Real-Life Example: HDR in Action

- **Before HDR**: A sunset photo shows an overexposed sky with washed-out colors and a dark foreground lacking detail.
- **After HDR**: The same photo reveals vibrant orange hues in the sky and visible textures in the foreground rocks.

Scene Optimization: AI-Powered Enhancements

What is Scene Optimization?

Scene Optimization uses AI to analyze your subject and environment, automatically adjusting settings like brightness, contrast, saturation, and white balance for optimal results. It simplifies complex photography techniques, making it accessible to all users.

When to Use Scene Optimization

1. **Portraits**:
   - Enhances skin tones while maintaining natural background colors.
   - Example: A sunny outdoor portrait where the AI balances light on the face without overexposing the background.
2. **Food Photography**:
   - Boosts saturation to make colors pop without oversaturation.
   - Example: A plate of colorful sushi under dim restaurant lighting.
3. **Night Photography**:
   - Brightens dark areas while reducing noise for sharper images.
   - Example: A cityscape at night showing vibrant lights without graininess.

Real-Life Example: Scene Optimization in Action

- **Before Scene Optimization**: A photo of a mural looks dull with muted colors due to uneven lighting.

- **After Scene Optimization**: The same photo showcases vibrant blues, greens, and oranges with balanced brightness across the frame.

How to Enable HDR and Scene Optimization on the Galaxy S25 Ultra

Step-by-Step Instructions:
1. Open the camera app on your Galaxy S25 Ultra.
2. Tap the settings icon (gear icon) at the top-left corner.
3. Enable HDR by toggling "Auto HDR" under Image Settings.
4. Activate Scene Optimization by toggling "Scene Optimizer" under Intelligent Features.

Comparison of Effects

Feature	Before Enhancement	After Enhancement
HDR	Overexposed highlights; dark shadows	Balanced brightness; visible details
Scene Optimization	Muted colors; uneven lighting	Vibrant hues; balanced exposure

Tips for Best Results
- Use HDR for static scenes where you can hold your phone steady during exposure blending.
- Rely on Scene Optimization for dynamic situations or when you need quick adjustments without manual tweaking.

By mastering these features, you can ensure every photo captured with your Samsung Galaxy S25 Ultra is vibrant, detailed, and professional-looking!

Chapter 4: Advanced Photography Features – Elevate Your Skills

The Samsung Galaxy S25 Ultra offers a range of advanced camera settings that can elevate your photography skills, allowing you to capture professional-quality photos with precision and creativity. This chapter delves into Pro Mode, explaining key settings like ISO, shutter speed, and white balance, along with practical examples to help you master these techniques.

Pro Mode Deep Dive: ISO, Shutter Speed, White Balance Explained

1. ISO Settings: Brightness and Noise Control

ISO controls the camera's sensitivity to light. Lower ISO values (e.g., ISO 100) are best for bright conditions or stationary subjects, while higher values (e.g., ISO 6400) are used for low-light conditions or moving subjects. However, high ISOs can introduce noise, which may degrade image quality.

Examples:

- **Low-Light Conditions**: Use a higher ISO (e.g., ISO 3200) to capture images in dim environments, but be aware that noise may increase.

- **Bright Conditions**: Use a lower ISO (e.g., ISO 100) to prevent overexposure and maintain image clarity.

2. Shutter Speed: Motion Blur and Action Freezing

Shutter speed determines how long the camera's shutter is open, affecting motion blur and the ability to freeze action.

Examples:

- **Sports Photography**: Use a fast shutter speed (e.g., 1/1000th of a second) to freeze fast-moving subjects like athletes.

- **Light Trails**: Employ a slow shutter speed (e.g., 30 seconds) to capture creative light trails from moving vehicles at night.

3. White Balance: Accurate Colors in Different Lighting Conditions

White balance adjusts the color temperature of your photos to match the lighting conditions, ensuring accurate and natural-looking colors.

Examples:

- **Daylight**: Use the "Daylight" or "Auto" white balance setting for outdoor shots to capture vibrant, natural colors.

- **Tungsten Lighting**: Select the "Tungsten" or "Incandescent" setting for indoor shots under artificial lighting to avoid yellowish hues.

- **Fluorescent Lighting**: Choose the "Fluorescent" setting to minimize greenish tones in office environments.

Practical Steps to Adjust These Settings in Pro Mode

1. **Access Pro Mode**:

- Open the camera app on your Galaxy S25 Ultra.

- Swipe to the "More" section and select "Pro Mode."

2. **Adjust ISO**:

- Tap the ISO icon and slide the bar to your desired sensitivity level.

3. **Adjust Shutter Speed**:

- Tap the shutter speed icon and select from available options or manually input a value.

4. **Adjust White Balance**:

- Tap the white balance icon and choose from presets like Daylight, Cloudy, Tungsten, or Fluorescent.

Real-World Examples and Tips

- **Night Sky Photography**: Use a low ISO (e.g., ISO 100) and slow shutter speed (e.g., 30 seconds) with manual focus for sharp stars.

- **Street Photography**: Employ a fast shutter speed (e.g., 1/500th of a second) and medium ISO (e.g., ISO 400) to capture sharp images of moving subjects.

By mastering these advanced settings in Pro Mode, you can unlock the full creative potential of your Galaxy S25 Ultra camera, ensuring every shot is a masterpiece!

RAW Photography Workflow for Professionals: Tips and Tricks

The Samsung Galaxy S25 Ultra empowers photographers with the ability to shoot in RAW format, unlocking unparalleled flexibility and creative control during post-processing. This section explores the benefits of RAW photography, guides you through enabling RAW mode on the Galaxy S25 Ultra, and provides tips for editing RAW files using built-in tools or third-party apps.

Benefits of Shooting in RAW Format

RAW photography captures unprocessed data directly from the camera sensor, preserving all details and tonal information for maximum editing flexibility. Unlike JPEGs, which compress and process images in-camera, RAW files act as "digital negatives," allowing photographers to refine every aspect of their photos.

Key Benefits:

1. **Enhanced Editing Flexibility**:

    o Adjust exposure, white balance, shadows, and highlights without degrading image quality.

    o Recover details in overexposed or underexposed areas for a balanced final image.

2. **Superior Image Quality**:

    o Retains richer color data and wider dynamic range compared to JPEGs.

o Ideal for professional-level prints or large-scale projects where detail matters.

3. **Non-Destructive Editing**:

   o Edits applied to RAW files do not alter the original data, ensuring you can revisit and refine your work without losing quality.

Step-by-Step Guide to Enabling RAW Mode on the Galaxy S25 Ultra

1. **Open Camera Settings**:

   o Launch the camera app and tap the settings icon (gear icon) at the top-left corner.

2. **Enable Pro Mode**:

   o Swipe to "More" in the mode selector and choose "Pro Mode."

3. **Activate RAW Format**:

   o In Pro Mode settings, toggle the option for "Save RAW + JPEG" under Image Format.

   o This saves both a compressed JPEG for quick sharing and a RAW file for advanced editing.

4. **Verify Storage Space**:

   o Ensure sufficient storage space is available, as RAW files are significantly larger than JPEGs.

Tips for Editing RAW Photos

Editing RAW files allows you to fine-tune every detail of your images. Here's how to make the most of your workflow:

Built-In Tools on the Galaxy S25 Ultra:

- Use Samsung's built-in photo editor for basic adjustments like exposure correction and color enhancement.

- Access advanced tools like highlights/shadows sliders directly within the gallery app.

Third-Party Apps:

1. **Adobe Lightroom**:
   - Import your RAW files into Lightroom for professional-grade editing.
   - Adjust exposure, contrast, white balance, and apply presets for consistent styles.
2. **Luminar Neo**:
   - Ideal for creative edits like AI-powered sky replacement or advanced color grading.
3. **Snapseed**:
   - A free app offering intuitive controls for fine-tuning brightness, saturation, and sharpness.

Editing Workflow:

1. Start with basic corrections:
   - Adjust exposure to balance highlights and shadows.
   - Set white balance according to lighting conditions (e.g., daylight or tungsten).

2. Refine details:
   - Use sharpening tools to enhance textures without introducing noise.
3. Apply creative adjustments:
   - Experiment with color grading or convert images to black-and-white for artistic effects.

Real-Life Examples

Scenario	Benefits of Shooting RAW	Editing Outcome
Landscape Photography	Recover shadow details in dark areas while preserving vibrant skies.	Balanced image with rich colors and textures.
Portraits	Correct skin tones using precise white balance adjustments.	Natural-looking portraits with accurate colors.
Night Photography	Reduce noise in low-light conditions while enhancing brightness.	Sharp night shots with minimal graininess.

Pro Tips

- Always shoot in RAW + JPEG mode for flexibility; use JPEGs for quick sharing while keeping RAW files for detailed edits.

- Organize your RAW files using cloud storage solutions like Google Drive or Dropbox to manage large file sizes efficiently.

By leveraging the Galaxy S25 Ultra's RAW capabilities and following this workflow, you can produce professional-grade photos that reflect your creative vision while maintaining exceptional quality.

Exclusive Tips for Using Depth Sensors and Bokeh Effects on the Samsung Galaxy S25 Ultra

The Samsung Galaxy S25 Ultra's advanced depth sensors and AI-powered camera system make it easy to create stunning bokeh effects, which beautifully blur the background while keeping your subject sharp. This section explains the role of depth sensors, provides step-by-step instructions for achieving professional-grade portraits with bokeh, and offers tips for optimizing aperture size and subject positioning.

Role of Depth Sensors in Creating Bokeh Effects

Depth sensors in the Galaxy S25 Ultra work by mapping the distance between the camera and various elements in the scene. This depth map allows the camera to distinguish between the foreground (your subject) and the background, applying a digital blur to areas outside the focus plane. The result is a creamy, out-of-focus background that enhances your subject's prominence.

How It Works:

- **Depth Mapping**: The sensor estimates the distance of each pixel from the camera, enabling precise segmentation of foreground and background.

- **AI Enhancements**: AI algorithms refine the blur effect, ensuring smooth transitions without harsh edges.

Step-by-Step Guide to Achieving Professional Bokeh Effects

1. **Activate Portrait Mode**:
   - Open the camera app on your Galaxy S25 Ultra.
   - Swipe to "Portrait Mode" in the mode selector.

2. **Position Your Subject**:
   - Place your subject at least 1-2 meters away from the camera.
   - Ensure there is significant distance between your subject and the background for stronger blur effects.

3. **Adjust Aperture Size**:
   - In Pro Mode, set a wide aperture (e.g., f/1.8) to create a shallow depth of field.
   - A wider aperture allows more light into the sensor, enhancing background blur.

4. **Fine-Tune Focus**:
   - Use manual focus if needed to ensure your subject is sharp.
   - Enable AI-assisted focus tracking for moving subjects.

5. **Experiment with Lighting**:
   - Use natural light during golden hour for soft highlights.

- o Add artificial light behind your subject for glowing bokeh effects (e.g., fairy lights).

6. **Capture Your Shot**:

    - o Tap to focus on your subject's eyes or face.

    - o Adjust framing to include blurred foreground elements for added depth.

Tips for Optimizing Bokeh Effects

1. **Increase Subject-Background Distance**:

    - o The greater the distance between your subject and the background, the stronger and smoother the blur effect.

2. **Use Longer Focal Lengths**:

    - o Zoom in using telephoto lenses (e.g., 3x or 5x optical zoom) to tighten depth of field and enhance bokeh quality.

3. **Incorporate Foreground Blur**:

    - o Position objects like leaves or flowers close to your camera lens to create a blurred foreground that frames your subject.

4. **Lighting Enhancements**:

    - o Bright highlights in the background (e.g., streetlights or candles) produce circular bokeh shapes that add artistic flair.

Advanced Photography Settings Cheat Sheet

Setting	Purpose	Recommended Values
ISO	Controls brightness/noise	ISO 100 (bright conditions), ISO 3200 (low light)
Shutter Speed	Freezes motion or creates blur	1/1000s (sports), 30s (light trails/night sky)
White Balance	Adjusts color temperature	Daylight (outdoors), Tungsten (indoor lighting)
Aperture Size	Creates shallow depth of field	f/1.8 (strong bokeh), f/5.6 (balanced focus)

Real-Life Example Comparisons

Example 1: Portrait with Depth Sensor

- **Before Depth Sensor Activation**: Background distractions compete with the subject.

- **After Depth Sensor Activation**: Smooth, blurred background highlights the subject's face.

Example 2: Creative Bokeh with Lights

- **Before Adjustment**: Background lights are sharp and distracting.

- **After Adjustment**: Lights transform into soft orbs, enhancing aesthetic appeal.

By leveraging these tips and settings on your Galaxy S25 Ultra, you can achieve stunning bokeh effects that rival professional DSLR results!

Chapter 5: Videography Mastery – Create Cinematic Content

Shooting in 8K vs. 4K: Which Resolution Is Right for You?

The Samsung Galaxy S25 Ultra offers both 8K and 4K video recording capabilities, giving users the flexibility to choose the best resolution for their needs. Understanding the differences between these resolutions will help you decide which one is ideal for your project, whether you're creating cinematic content or quick social media clips.

Resolution Comparison: 8K vs. 4K

Feature	8K Resolution	4K Resolution
Pixel Count	7,680 x 4,320 (33 million pixels)	3,840 x 2,160 (8.3 million pixels)
Detail Level	Ultra-sharp and lifelike; ideal for large screens	High clarity; excellent for most viewing devices
File Size	Larger; requires significant storage space	Smaller; more manageable file sizes
Processing Power	Demands higher processing power	Easier to edit and render
Use Cases	Cinematic shots, professional projects	Social media, YouTube, everyday videos

Key Differences Explained

1. **Detail and Clarity**:

   o **8K Resolution**: Offers four times the detail of 4K, making it ideal for large screens or projects that require extreme sharpness. Perfect for cinematic shots where every detail matters.

   o **4K Resolution**: Still delivers excellent clarity and detail but is more practical for most devices and platforms.

2. **File Size and Storage**:

   o Recording in 8K generates significantly larger files due to the increased pixel count. This requires more storage space and faster processing speeds during editing.

   o In contrast, 4K files are smaller and easier to manage, making them suitable for everyday use.

3. **Content Compatibility**:

   o While 8K is cutting-edge technology, most platforms (e.g., YouTube, Instagram) currently optimize content for 4K or lower resolutions.

   o Use 4K for content intended for social media or general sharing.

Recommendations Based on Use Cases

When to Choose 8K

- **Cinematic Content**: Ideal for professional projects like short films or commercials where ultra-high detail is required.

- **Future-Proofing**: If you plan to archive your footage or use it on next-gen displays, 8K ensures your content remains relevant.

- **Large Screens**: Perfect for playback on large displays where higher pixel density enhances viewing quality.

When to Choose 4K

- **Social Media Videos**: Optimized for platforms like Instagram and YouTube where file size and compatibility matter.

- **Everyday Use**: Great for capturing family moments, travel vlogs, or quick edits.

- **Efficient Editing**: Easier to process on standard editing software without requiring high-end hardware.

How to Switch Between Resolutions on the Galaxy S25 Ultra

1. Open the camera app and select "Video Mode."

2. Tap the settings icon (gear icon) at the top-left corner.

3. Navigate to "Resolution" under video settings.

4. Choose between:

   o **8K UHD (30fps)** for ultra-high-definition cinematic shots.

- **4K UHD (60fps)** for smoother motion and high-quality everyday videos.

Tips for Shooting in Each Resolution

Shooting in 8K:

- Ensure ample storage space before recording.

- Use a tripod or gimbal to stabilize footage; even minor movements are noticeable at higher resolutions.

- Plan post-production carefully as rendering times will be longer due to file size.

Shooting in 4K:

- Utilize higher frame rates (e.g., 60fps) for smoother action sequences.

- Ideal for handheld shots due to manageable file size and easier stabilization during editing.

By understanding the strengths of both resolutions available on the Samsung Galaxy S25 Ultra, you can tailor your videography approach to suit your creative goals — whether you're crafting cinematic masterpieces or quick social media content!

Advanced Stabilization Techniques: Super Steady & OIS

The Samsung Galaxy S25 Ultra features advanced stabilization technologies, including **Super Steady mode** and **Optical Image Stabilization (OIS)**, designed to minimize camera shake and ensure smoother video recording. These tools are particularly useful for handheld recording, zoomed-in shots, and low-light conditions.

Super Steady Mode: Reducing Shake During Handheld Recording

Super Steady mode is an action camera function that uses advanced algorithms to stabilize footage, especially when moving at high speeds. It effectively crops in from the main camera sensor and applies digital stabilization to counteract camera motion, making it ideal for capturing smooth video while running, biking, or following fast-moving subjects.

How It Works:

- **Digital Stabilization**: Super Steady uses software to analyze and adjust the video feed in real-time, compensating for camera movements.

- **Cropped Footage**: It crops into the frame slightly to allow for more aggressive stabilization, which can result in a slightly reduced field of view.

Example:

- **Non-Stabilized Footage**: A video recorded while running shows noticeable shake and blur.

- **Super Steady Footage**: The same scene recorded with Super Steady mode appears smooth and stable, as if shot with a gimbal.

Optical Image Stabilization (OIS): Benefits for Zoomed-In Shots and Low-Light Conditions

OIS is a hardware-based stabilization system that physically adjusts the camera lens to counteract camera movements. This technology is particularly effective for zoomed-in shots and low-light conditions where camera shake can be more pronounced.

Benefits:

1. **Zoomed-In Shots**: OIS helps maintain sharpness and stability when using telephoto lenses (3x or 5x zoom), ensuring that distant subjects remain clear and focused.

2. **Low-Light Conditions**: By reducing camera motion, OIS minimizes blur caused by slower shutter speeds in dim environments, resulting in sharper images.

Example:

- **Non-OIS Footage**: A zoomed-in video shot in low light shows noticeable blur due to camera shake.

- **OIS Footage**: The same shot with OIS enabled remains sharp and stable, capturing clear details even in low-light conditions.

Enabling Super Steady and OIS on the Galaxy S25 Ultra

1. **Super Steady Mode**:

    o   Open the camera app and select "Video Mode."

    o   Tap the Super Steady icon to enable it. Note that Super Steady may reduce shutter speeds and is best used in well-lit conditions.

2. **Optical Image Stabilization (OIS)**:

    o   OIS is automatically enabled for supported lenses (e.g., telephoto lenses).

    o   Ensure that your camera settings are optimized for low-light conditions or zoomed shots.

Tips for Enhanced Stabilization

- **Use a Tripod or Gimbal**: For maximum stability, especially when recording at higher zoom levels or in low light.

- **Adjust Resolution and Frame Rate**: Lowering these settings can help reduce file size and improve stabilization during editing.

- **Install Camera Assistant Apps**: Tools like Good Lock can offer additional stabilization options and fine-tune camera settings for better results.

By leveraging Super Steady mode and OIS on your Galaxy S25 Ultra, you can capture incredibly smooth and stable footage, even in challenging conditions!

Frame Rate Control for Dynamic Videos: Tips for Smooth Footage

The Samsung Galaxy S25 Ultra offers versatile frame rate options, including **30fps**, **60fps**, and higher, allowing users to tailor their video recordings to specific needs. Understanding frame rate differences is key to achieving smooth, high-quality footage. Here's a breakdown of how frame rates impact video quality and motion smoothness, along with recommendations for different use cases.

Understanding Frame Rate Options

Frame Rate	Characteristics	Best Use Cases
30fps	Standard frame rate; smooth and natural motion	Casual filming, vlogs, social media videos
60fps	Higher frame rate; smoother motion and details	Action scenes, sports, gaming content
120fps+	Ultra-high frame rate; ideal for slow-motion effects	Cinematic slow-motion, creative shots

Impact on Video Quality and Motion Smoothness

1. **30fps**:

   - Captures 30 frames per second, providing smooth motion for everyday video recording.

   - Ideal for standard content creation like vlogs or interviews.

   - Example: A casual walk-through of a location with natural movement.

2. **60fps**:

   - Captures twice as many frames per second as 30fps, resulting in smoother transitions and sharper details in fast-moving scenes.

   - Perfect for high-motion activities like sports or action sequences.

   - Example: Recording a skateboarder performing tricks with fluid motion.

3. **120fps or Higher**:

   - Captures ultra-high-speed footage that can be slowed down to create dramatic slow-motion effects.

   - Ideal for cinematic shots or creative storytelling.

   - Example: A water droplet falling into a pond slowed down to reveal intricate ripples.

Choosing the Right Frame Rate Based on Use Cases

When to Use 30fps

- **Standard Recording**: Great for everyday videos where natural motion is sufficient.

- **Social Media Content**: Compatible with platforms like Instagram and YouTube without requiring excessive storage or processing power.

When to Use 60fps

- **Action Scenes**: Smooths out fast-paced motion, making it ideal for sports or dynamic events.

- **Gaming Content**: Enhances clarity in high-motion gaming footage.

When to Use 120fps+

- **Slow-Motion Effects**: Allows you to slow down footage dramatically while maintaining smooth transitions.

- **Cinematic Shots**: Adds an artistic flair to storytelling by emphasizing details in fast-moving elements.

How to Adjust Frame Rates on the Galaxy S25 Ultra

1. Open the camera app and select "Video Mode."

2. Tap the settings icon (gear icon) at the top-left corner.

3. Navigate to "Resolution and Frame Rate."

4. Choose your desired resolution (e.g., 4K or 1080p) and frame rate:

   o Select 30fps for standard recording.

   o Select 60fps for smoother motion in high-action scenes.

o Select 120fps or higher for slow-motion effects.

Real-Life Examples of Frame Rate Choices

1. **Sports Event Recording (60fps):**

   o Capturing a soccer match ensures smooth transitions as players move across the field without motion blur.

2. **Slow-Motion Waterfall (120fps):**

   o Slowing down footage reveals intricate water flows and splashes that are invisible at standard speeds.

3. **Casual Vlog (30fps):**

   o Walking through a park with natural movement feels more relatable and requires less storage space than higher frame rates.

Tips for Optimizing Frame Rates

- Use higher frame rates (e.g., 60fps or 120fps) when recording fast-moving subjects or when planning slow-motion edits.

- Stick to 30fps for casual videos intended for quick sharing on social media platforms.

- Ensure adequate storage space when using higher frame rates, as larger files are generated.

By mastering frame rate control on your Galaxy S25 Ultra, you can create dynamic videos tailored to your creative vision — whether capturing cinematic slow-motion or smooth action-packed moments!

Travel Photography Tips with Ultra-Wide Lenses: Capturing Landscapes

The Samsung Galaxy S25 Ultra's **50MP ultra-wide lens** is a game-changer for travel photography, especially when capturing breathtaking landscapes. This lens allows you to capture expansive vistas with incredible detail and depth, making it perfect for sweeping mountain ranges, vast deserts, or sprawling cityscapes. Here's how to maximize its potential and create stunning travel shots.

How the Ultra-Wide Lens Enhances Landscape Photography

1. **Capturing More Detail and Depth**:

- The 50MP ultra-wide lens offers higher resolution than its predecessors, ensuring that every element in your landscape — whether it's a distant mountain peak or a foreground rock — is captured with clarity.

- The **f/1.9 aperture** allows more light into the sensor, improving low-light performance and enhancing the dynamic range of your shots.

2. **Composition Techniques**:

- **Leading Lines**: Use roads, paths, or shorelines to guide the viewer's eye into the frame, creating depth and perspective.

- **Rule of Thirds**: Divide your image into thirds both horizontally and vertically. Place interesting features along these lines to create balanced compositions.

- Symmetry: Look for symmetrical elements like reflections or archways to add visual interest.

Tips for Stunning Travel Shots

1. **Shoot During Golden Hour**:

   - The soft, warm light of early morning or late afternoon enhances colors and textures, making landscapes more vibrant.

   - Example: A mountain range at sunrise with golden hues on the peaks.

2. **Experiment with Angles**:

   - Shoot from low or high vantage points to add drama to your landscapes.

   - Example: A low-angle shot of a skyscraper to emphasize its height.

3. **Incorporate Foreground Elements**:

   - Use objects like rocks, trees, or buildings to frame your scene and add depth.

   - Example: A tree in the foreground with a mountain range in the background.

4. **Utilize the Ultra-Wide Lens for Panoramic Shots**:

   - Capture expansive views by stitching multiple ultra-wide shots together.

   - Example: A panoramic view of a city skyline at dusk.

Real-Life Examples

1. **Ultra-Wide Landscape**:

   o Capture a sweeping beach scene with the ultra-wide lens, showcasing the vastness of the ocean and surrounding landscape.

   o Tip: Use leading lines like the shoreline to guide the viewer's eye.

2. **Macro Photography with Ultra-Wide Lens**:

   o Experiment with close-up shots of textures or patterns using the ultra-wide lens's autofocus capabilities.

   o Example: A close-up of intricate rock formations or a flower.

By leveraging the Galaxy S25 Ultra's ultra-wide lens and applying these composition techniques, you can create stunning travel landscapes that capture the essence of your adventures. Whether you're exploring new cities or hiking through nature reserves, these tips will help you preserve your memories in breathtaking detail!

Chapter 6: Travel Photography Tips with Ultra-Wide Lenses: Capturing Landscapes

The Samsung Galaxy S25 Ultra's **50MP ultra-wide lens** is a game-changer for travel photography, especially when capturing breathtaking landscapes. This lens allows you to capture expansive vistas with incredible detail and depth, making it perfect for sweeping mountain ranges, vast deserts, or sprawling cityscapes. Here's how to maximize its potential and create stunning travel shots.

How the Ultra-Wide Lens Enhances Landscape Photography

1. **Capturing More Detail and Depth**:

   o The 50MP ultra-wide lens offers higher resolution than its predecessors, ensuring that every element in your landscape—whether it's a distant mountain peak or a foreground rock—is captured with clarity.

   o The **f/1.9 aperture** allows more light into the sensor, improving low-light performance and enhancing the dynamic range of your shots.

2. **Composition Techniques**:

   o **Leading Lines**: Use roads, paths, or shorelines to guide the viewer's eye into the frame, creating depth and perspective.

o **Rule of Thirds**: Divide your image into thirds both horizontally and vertically. Place interesting features along these lines to create balanced compositions.

o **Symmetry**: Look for symmetrical elements like reflections or archways to add visual interest.

Tips for Stunning Travel Shots

1. **Shoot During Golden Hour**:

   o The soft, warm light of early morning or late afternoon enhances colors and textures, making landscapes more vibrant.

   o Example: A mountain range at sunrise with golden hues on the peaks.

2. **Experiment with Angles**:

   o Shoot from low or high vantage points to add drama to your landscapes.

   o Example: A low-angle shot of a skyscraper to emphasize its height.

3. **Incorporate Foreground Elements**:

   o Use objects like rocks, trees, or buildings to frame your scene and add depth.

   o Example: A tree in the foreground with a mountain range in the background.

4. **Utilize the Ultra-Wide Lens for Panoramic Shots**:

- Capture expansive views by stitching multiple ultra-wide shots together.

- Example: A panoramic view of a city skyline at dusk.

Real-Life Examples

1. **Ultra-Wide Landscape**:

   - Capture a sweeping beach scene with the ultra-wide lens, showcasing the vastness of the ocean and surrounding landscape.

   - Tip: Use leading lines like the shoreline to guide the viewer's eye.

2. **Macro Photography with Ultra-Wide Lens**:

   - Experiment with close-up shots of textures or patterns using the ultra-wide lens's autofocus capabilities.

   - Example: A close-up of intricate rock formations or a flower.

By leveraging the Galaxy S25 Ultra's ultra-wide lens and applying these composition techniques, you can create stunning travel landscapes that capture the essence of your adventures. Whether you're exploring new cities or hiking through nature reserves, these tips will help you preserve your memories in breathtaking detail!

Food Photography Tricks for Vibrant Colors in Dim Lighting: Styling and Setup

Capturing vibrant food photos in dim lighting requires a combination of clever lighting techniques, attractive styling, and thoughtful setup. Here's how to enhance your food photography using natural light, reflective surfaces, and creative styling tips.

Lighting Techniques for Vibrant Colors

1. **Natural Light**:

    o Position your setup near a window to utilize soft, diffused natural light. This is ideal for creating warm tones and gentle shadows.

    o Use sheer curtains to soften harsh direct sunlight if needed.

2. **Artificial Lighting**:

- Employ a single light source with a softbox or diffuser to create soft shadows and emphasize textures. This setup is versatile for both bright and moody effects.

- Side lighting or backlighting can add depth and dimension to your dishes, highlighting colors and textures.

3. **Reflective Surfaces**:

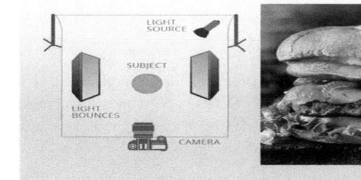

- Use reflectors (e.g., white cardboard or aluminum foil) to bounce light onto darker areas, ensuring consistent illumination and vibrant colors.

- Avoid overusing reflectors to maintain shadows that add depth to your images.

Styling Tips for Visually Appealing Food Photos

1. **Arrange Dishes Attractively**:

   - Balance elements on the plate to create visual harmony. Consider the rule of thirds for placement.

   - Use garnishes like fresh herbs or edible flowers to add pops of color.

2. **Incorporate Props**:

   - Add context with props like vintage utensils, linens, or wooden boards to create a cozy atmosphere.

   - Use props to frame your dish or add depth to the scene.

3. **Background Selection**:

   - Choose backgrounds that complement your dish's colors. Dark backgrounds can make vibrant colors stand out, while light backgrounds can create a clean look.

   - Experiment with textures like wood or marble for added visual interest.

Setup Examples for Dim Lighting Conditions

1. **Dark and Moody Setup**:

   o Use a single light source with a diffuser to create soft shadows. Position black foam core to absorb light and enhance contrast.

   o This setup is ideal for emphasizing textures and creating dramatic effects.

2. **Bright and Airy Setup**:

   o Position your setup near a window with sheer curtains to soften the light.

   o Use a reflector to fill in shadows and maintain vibrant colors.

Real-Life Examples

1. **Vibrant Fruit Salad**:

   o Arrange colorful fruits on a dark background with a single light source positioned at an angle to highlight textures and colors.

   o Add fresh herbs as garnishes for added vibrancy.

2. **Moody Coffee Shot**:

   o Use a dark background and side lighting to create deep shadows. Position a coffee cup on a wooden board with steam rising to add drama.

Tips for Capturing in Dim Conditions

- **Invest in Artificial Lighting**: Softboxes or LED panels can provide consistent lighting when natural light is limited.

- **Experiment with Angles**: Shoot from different angles to add visual interest and depth to your images.

- **Emphasize Shadows**: Don't be afraid to leave some shadows in your image; they add depth and dimension.

By combining these lighting techniques with thoughtful styling and setup, you can create stunning food photos even in dim lighting conditions!

Social Media Content Creation Made Easy: Tips for Engaging Photos

Creating eye-catching social media content with engaging photos is essential for capturing attention and boosting engagement. The Samsung Galaxy S25 Ultra's advanced camera features, combined with thoughtful framing, editing, and branding techniques, make it easy to produce standout visuals optimized for platforms like Instagram and TikTok.

Framing Techniques for Eye-Catching Photos

1. **Rule of Thirds**:

   o Divide your frame into nine equal sections using a grid. Place your subject along the intersecting lines for balanced and visually appealing compositions.

   o Example: Position a coffee cup slightly off-center with natural light streaming in from the side.

2. **Leading Lines**:

   o Use natural lines (e.g., roads, fences, or table edges) to guide the viewer's eye toward your subject.

- Example: A plate of food framed by utensils leading toward the dish.

3. **Negative Space**:

   - Incorporate empty space around your subject to emphasize its importance and create a clean aesthetic.

   - Example: A minimalist photo of a single flower on a blank background.

Filters and Editing Tools

1. **Filters**:

   - Use subtle filters to enhance colors without over-editing. Warm tones work well for food photography, while cooler tones suit travel or lifestyle shots.

   - Example: Apply a soft vintage filter to a cityscape for an artistic touch.

2. **Editing Tools**:

   - Use built-in editing tools on the Galaxy S25 Ultra or apps like Adobe Lightroom or Snapseed to adjust brightness, contrast, and saturation.

   - Example: Increase brightness and sharpen details in dimly lit food photos.

Consistency in Style and Branding

1. **Signature Style**:

- o Develop a consistent visual style that aligns with your brand identity. This includes color palettes, filters, and composition techniques.

- o Example: Use pastel tones and soft lighting for lifestyle content to create a cohesive feed.

2. **Branding Elements**:

- o Incorporate subtle branding elements like logos or consistent fonts in graphics to reinforce your identity without overwhelming the image.

- o Example: Add your brand name in a small corner of each image.

Practical Examples for Social Media Content

1. **Travel Photos**:

- o Use the ultra-wide lens to capture expansive landscapes with leading lines guiding the viewer's eye.

- o Example: A sunset shot with a winding road leading toward the horizon.

2. **Food Photography**:

- o Style dishes attractively using props like linens or utensils for context. Enhance colors using reflective surfaces or artificial lighting.

- o Example: A vibrant salad shot with garnishes framed by rustic wooden boards.

3. **Lifestyle Shots**:

- Incorporate candid moments or behind-the-scenes imagery to add authenticity.
- Example: A casual photo of someone enjoying coffee at home.

Tips for Optimized Social Media Content

- **Post Regularly**: Aim for at least 3 posts per week to maintain engagement.
- **Keep It Simple**: Avoid cluttered designs; focus on clean compositions that highlight key elements.
- **Engage Your Audience**: Include captions that tell a story or ask questions to encourage interaction.

By combining thoughtful framing techniques, consistent branding, and smart editing tools, you can create engaging social media content that stands out on platforms like Instagram and TikTok!

Platform-Specific Optimization

Creating content optimized for specific social media platforms ensures better engagement and visibility. Each platform has unique requirements, trends, and audience preferences, so tailoring your approach can make your posts stand out. Here's a detailed guide for Instagram, TikTok, and Pinterest.

Instagram: Visual Storytelling with Balanced Composition

Instagram is a visual-first platform where aesthetics and storytelling play a major role. Optimizing your posts for its feed, Stories, and Reels can help maximize reach and engagement.

Aspect Ratios

- **Feed Posts**: Use a 4:5 (portrait) aspect ratio for photos and videos. It takes up more screen space on mobile devices, grabbing the viewer's attention.

    o Example: A travel photo of a waterfall framed vertically to showcase its height and grandeur.

- **Stories & Reels**: Use 9:16 (full-screen portrait) for immersive content that fills the viewer's screen.

    o Example: A food preparation video shot vertically to highlight every detail.

Hashtags

- Use relevant hashtags to improve discoverability. Combine niche hashtags (#FoodStylingTips) with popular ones (#TravelPhotography) to reach both targeted and broader audiences.

- Limit hashtags to 15–20 per post to avoid clutter while maximizing visibility.

Carousel Posts

- Create multi-image posts to tell a story or showcase different perspectives of the same subject.

    o Example: A carousel post showing a travel destination from various angles—wide shots, close-ups, and candid moments.

- Include a call-to-action in the last slide (e.g., "Swipe to see the full transformation!").

TikTok: Dynamic Content for Viral Engagement

TikTok thrives on short-form, engaging content that captures attention within seconds. Leveraging trends and creative tools can help you create viral-worthy videos.

Dynamic Content

- Use transitions like quick cuts, zoom-ins, or object reveals to keep viewers engaged.

   o Example: A travel video transitioning from packing bags to arriving at a scenic destination.

- Incorporate movement—record walking tours or panning shots using the Galaxy S25 Ultra's **Super Steady mode** for smooth footage.

Trendy Sounds

- Pair your videos with trending audio tracks or music to boost discoverability through TikTok's algorithm.

   o Example: Use upbeat music for a food preparation video or calming sounds for nature-focused travel clips.

- Regularly explore TikTok's "Discover" page to identify trending sounds relevant to your niche.

Text Overlays

- Add text overlays directly in TikTok or during editing to provide context or call-to-action messages.

- Example: Overlay "5 Must-Try Foods in Paris" on a food montage video.

- Use bold fonts and contrasting colors to ensure readability against dynamic backgrounds.

Pinterest: Shareable Content with Informative Graphics

Pinterest is ideal for evergreen content that inspires users or provides practical information. Optimizing pins with vertical orientation and text overlays can increase their shareability.

Vertical Orientation

- Use a 2:3 aspect ratio (e.g., 1000x1500 pixels) for photos and graphics. Vertical pins stand out on Pinterest feeds compared to square or horizontal images.

  - Example: A pin showcasing a travel itinerary with scenic landmarks arranged vertically.

Text Graphics

- Add text overlays that provide context or actionable information — like tutorials, recipes, or tips.

  - Example: A pin titled "10 Easy Food Styling Tricks" with step-by-step visuals of styled dishes.

- Ensure text is legible by using clean fonts and placing it against uncluttered backgrounds.

Additional Tips Across Platforms

1. **Consistency in Branding**:

- o Maintain cohesive aesthetics across platforms by using similar filters, color palettes, and fonts. This strengthens your visual identity.

2. **Engage Your Audience**:

- o Include interactive elements like polls in Instagram Stories or questions in TikTok captions to encourage participation.

3. **Optimize Posting Times**:

- o Post when your audience is most active — typically evenings for Instagram and weekends for Pinterest.

4. **Leverage Analytics**:

- o Use platform insights (e.g., Instagram Insights or Pinterest Analytics) to track engagement metrics and refine content strategies.

Leveraging AI Features on the Galaxy S25 Ultra

The Samsung Galaxy S25 Ultra is equipped with advanced AI-powered tools that simplify content creation while enhancing the quality of your photos and videos. These features are especially useful for crafting professional-looking content for social media platforms like Instagram, TikTok, and Pinterest. Here's how you can take advantage of these AI features:

Scene Optimization

The Scene Optimization feature uses AI to automatically adjust settings like brightness, contrast, color saturation, and exposure based on the subject and environment. It recognizes various scenarios—such as food, landscapes, or portraits—and fine-tunes the image to make it more visually appealing.

How to Use Scene Optimization:

1. Open the camera app.

2. Ensure "Scene Optimizer" is enabled in the settings.

3. Point your camera at your subject, and the AI will automatically detect the scene type and apply enhancements.

Example:

- **Before**: A photo of a plate of pasta looks dull with muted colors in low light.

- **After**: Scene Optimization boosts saturation to make the red sauce pop and adjusts brightness for a vibrant, appetizing look.

Object Eraser

The Object Eraser tool allows you to remove unwanted elements from your photos directly in the gallery app. Whether it's a distracting photobomber or clutter in the background, this feature ensures your subject remains the focal point.

How to Use Object Eraser:

1. Open a photo in the gallery app.

2. Tap "Edit" and select "Object Eraser."

3. Highlight or tap on the object you want to remove, and let AI seamlessly fill in the background.

Example:

- **Before**: A travel photo of a scenic beach has people in the background distracting from the serene view.

- **After**: Object Eraser removes the people, leaving a clean and tranquil beach scene.

Live Focus Video

Live Focus Video adds depth-of-field effects to your videos by blurring the background while keeping your subject in sharp focus. This feature creates a cinematic look that's perfect for Instagram Reels or TikTok videos.

How to Use Live Focus Video:

1. Open the camera app and switch to "Video Mode."

2. Select "Live Focus Video" from the available options.

3. Adjust the intensity of the background blur using the slider before or during recording.

Example:

- Record a TikTok video where you're showcasing an outfit while blurring out a messy room in the background for a polished, professional vibe.

Engaging Captions and Call-to-Actions (CTAs)

Photos and videos are only part of what makes social media content engaging—captions play a critical role in connecting with your audience and driving interaction. A well-crafted caption can tell a story, evoke emotion, or inspire action.

Storytelling Captions

Captions that share personal stories or behind-the-scenes moments help create an emotional connection with your audience. These captions make your posts feel authentic and relatable, encouraging followers to engage with your content.

Tips for Storytelling Captions:

- Keep it concise but meaningful.

- Share a moment that complements your photo or video.

- End with an open-ended question to spark conversation.

Example:

"This shot was taken moments before sunset at my favorite beach — can you guess where? The colors were so vibrant I almost didn't need any filters! Let me know if this reminds you of your favorite travel spot."

Interactive CTAs

Interactive CTAs encourage your audience to participate by asking questions, prompting actions, or inviting feedback. This not only boosts engagement but also helps build a sense of community around your content.

Tips for Interactive CTAs:

- Ask specific questions related to your post.

- Encourage followers to share their opinions or experiences.

- Use action words like "comment," "swipe," "vote," or "tag."

Example:

"Which dish looks more delicious? Swipe left to see both options and let me know in the comments! "

Combining AI Features with Captions

By pairing AI-enhanced visuals with engaging captions, you can create social media posts that are both visually striking and interactive. For example:

1. Use Scene Optimization to enhance colors in a food photo.

2. Write a storytelling caption about how you discovered the dish.

3. Add an interactive CTA like: *"What's your go-to comfort food? Comment below!"*

These tools and techniques will help you craft content that stands out while fostering meaningful engagement with your audience!

Using Motion and Transitions

Motion and transitions are crucial for creating engaging content on platforms like TikTok and Instagram Reels, where dynamic visuals capture attention in seconds. The Samsung Galaxy S25 Ultra's advanced video capabilities, such as Super Steady mode, make it easy to incorporate smooth motion and creative transitions for professional-quality videos.

Smooth Panning Shots

Smooth panning shots are perfect for adding movement to your videos, whether you're showcasing a product, a location, or a process. The Galaxy S25 Ultra's **Super Steady mode** ensures fluid motion even when recording handheld.

How to Create Smooth Panning Shots:

1. Open the camera app and switch to **Video Mode**.

2. Enable **Super Steady mode** by tapping the hand icon at the top of the screen.

3. Slowly move your phone horizontally or vertically while keeping your subject in focus.

Example:

4. Record a travel video where you pan across a scenic landscape, such as a mountain range or beach, to highlight its vastness.

Creative Transitions

Transitions make your videos visually engaging by seamlessly connecting different clips. Instagram Reels and TikTok both support creative transitions that can be enhanced with the Galaxy S25 Ultra's features.

Transition Techniques:

1. **Zoom-Ins**: Use the camera's zoom slider to smoothly transition into a close-up of your subject.

   o Example: Start with a wide shot of a dish and zoom in to reveal intricate details of its presentation.

2. **Quick Cuts**: Record short clips of different scenes and edit them together for fast-paced storytelling.

   o Example: A "day in the life" video showing quick snippets of morning coffee, work setup, and evening relaxation.

3. **Object Reveals**: Use an object (e.g., your hand or a prop) to cover the lens between clips for seamless transitions.

   o Example: Cover the lens with your hand at the end of one clip, then start the next clip by uncovering it in a new location.

Pro Tip:

4. Use Instagram's built-in transition effects (e.g., warp or swirl) for added flair. Access these effects by tapping the **Sparkle icon** in Reels Create mode.

Analytics and Insights

Tracking performance metrics is essential for refining your content strategy. Both Instagram and TikTok provide built-in analytics tools that offer valuable insights into audience behavior, engagement rates, and content performance.

How to Use Analytics Tools

Instagram Insights:

1. Switch to a professional account (if not already done).

2. Go to your profile and tap the menu icon (three lines).

3. Select "Insights" to view metrics like:

    o Reach: The number of unique accounts that saw your content.

    o Engagement: Likes, comments, shares, and saves.

    o Audience Demographics: Age, gender, location, and active times.

TikTok Analytics:

4. Switch to a Pro Account under "Manage Account" settings.

5. Access analytics from your profile menu to view:

    o Video Performance: Total views, likes, comments, shares.

    o Follower Activity: Peak times when your audience is most active.

Refining Your Content Strategy

1. **Experiment with Posting Times**:

    o Use analytics to determine when your audience is most active and post during those times for maximum reach.

    o Example: If analytics show peak activity at 7 PM, schedule posts around that time.

2. **Identify High-Performing Content**:

- Analyze which posts have the highest engagement rates and replicate their style or format.

- Example: If travel Reels with smooth panning shots perform well, create more content using similar techniques.

3. **Test Different Formats**:

- Alternate between short-form videos (7–15 seconds) for quick engagement and slightly longer videos (30–60 seconds) for storytelling.

Practical Tips for Motion & Analytics

- Combine smooth motion techniques with trending audio tracks on TikTok or Instagram Reels for better algorithmic visibility.

- Use captions or text overlays in Reels to make content accessible for viewers who watch without sound.

- Monitor performance regularly and adjust based on audience preferences — consistency paired with data-driven adjustments leads to growth.

Collaborative Content

Social media thrives on collaboration, allowing creators to expand their reach, engage with new audiences, and experiment with fresh ideas. The Samsung Galaxy S25 Ultra's features, combined with creative collaboration strategies, make it easy to produce compelling co-branded content. Here's how to leverage collaborations effectively:

Partnering with Influencers or Friends

Collaborating with influencers or friends can help you tap into their audience while showcasing your brand in a relatable way.

Ideas for Collaborative Posts:

1. **Co-Branded Content**:

   o Share a joint post featuring both parties using products or services.

   o Example: Partner with a food influencer to create a recipe video featuring your product.

2. **Social Media Takeovers**:

   o Allow collaborators to post on your account for a day, sharing behind-the-scenes content or Q&A sessions.

   o Example: A travel blogger takes over your Instagram Stories to showcase a destination using your Galaxy S25 Ultra.

Dual-Camera Features for Creative Collaborations

The Galaxy S25 Ultra's dual-camera functionality enables innovative collaborative content by capturing multiple perspectives simultaneously.

How to Use Dual-Camera Features:

1. Enable Dual Recording in the camera app.

2. Record using both the front and rear cameras to capture reactions alongside the scene.

3. Combine clips during editing for a dynamic storytelling effect.

Example:

4. Collaborate with a friend to create a travel vlog where one camera captures the landscape and the other records personal reactions.

Creative Collaboration Ideas

1. **Live Interviews**:

   o Host live Q&A sessions or interviews with collaborators using Instagram Live or TikTok Live.

2. **Shared Giveaways**:

   o Partner with another creator or brand for giveaways that appeal to both audiences.

   o Example: A tech influencer and a travel blogger collaborate on a giveaway featuring the Galaxy S25 Ultra and travel accessories.

3. **Video Stitches**:

   o Use TikTok's stitch feature to respond to or build upon another creator's video.

Editing Apps Recommendations

While the Galaxy S25 Ultra offers robust built-in editing tools, third-party apps provide even more creative freedom for refining your social media content.

Recommended Apps

Canva

- Perfect for creating graphics, text overlays, and branded templates.

- Features drag-and-drop designs ideal for Instagram Stories, Pinterest pins, and TikTok thumbnails.

- Example: Create a visually appealing infographic summarizing travel tips using Canva.

VSCO

- Offers professional-grade filters and advanced photo editing tools like exposure adjustments and color grading.

- Ideal for maintaining consistency in style across posts.

- Example: Apply VSCO filters to create a cohesive aesthetic for food photography posts.

InShot

- A user-friendly video editor that allows you to add transitions, text effects, and music tracks.

- Perfect for TikTok or Instagram Reels where dynamic edits are key to engagement.

- Example: Edit a travel montage with smooth transitions and trending audio tracks using InShot.

Tips for Using Editing Apps

1. Stick to consistent color palettes and fonts across Canva designs for branding cohesion.

2. Use VSCO presets to ensure all photos share similar tones and styles.

3. Experiment with InShot's transition effects (e.g., zoom cuts or fades) to make videos visually engaging.

By combining collaborative strategies like influencer partnerships and dual-camera features with powerful editing apps like Canva, VSCO, and InShot, you can create high-quality social media content that resonates with audiences while expanding your reach!

Chapter 7: Editing Like a Pro - Tools and Techniques

The Samsung Galaxy S25 Ultra offers powerful built-in editing tools and advanced third-party app compatibility, enabling users to edit photos professionally with ease. This chapter explores the editing tools available on the device, focusing on cropping, adjusting brightness/contrast, enhancing colors, and saving images in different formats. Tutorials and examples are included to help you master these features.

Built-in Editing Tools Explored

The Galaxy S25 Ultra's editing tools provide intuitive controls for refining your photos directly in the gallery app. These tools include cropping, brightness adjustment, contrast enhancement, and more.

Cropping, brightness adjustment, contrast enhancement, and more.

1. Cropping

Cropping allows you to remove unwanted areas of your photo and focus on the subject for better composition. **Step-by-Step Tutorial**:

1. Open the **Gallery** app and select the photo you want to edit.

2. Tap the **Edit** icon (pencil icon) at the bottom of the screen.

3. Select the **Crop** tool.

4. Drag the corners or edges of the crop box to adjust the frame.

5. Tap **Save** to apply changes. **Example**:

6. Before: A landscape photo with distracting elements on the edges.

7. After: Cropped to focus on the central mountain range.

2. Adjusting Brightness and Contrast

Brightness and contrast adjustments ensure your photo has balanced lighting and depth. **Step-by-Step Tutorial**:

1. Open a photo in the **Gallery** app.

2. Tap the **Edit** icon and select **Adjust**.

3. Use sliders to increase or decrease brightness and contrast.

4. Preview changes in real-time before saving. **Example**:

5. Before: A dimly lit food photo with muted colors.

6. After: Brightened with enhanced contrast for vibrant tones.

3. Enhancing Colors

Enhancing colors makes your photos pop by adjusting saturation, warmth, or vibrancy. **Step-by-Step Tutorial**:

1. Open a photo in the **Gallery** app.

2. Tap **Edit**, then select **Filters or Adjust Colors**.

3. Use sliders to tweak saturation, warmth, or color balance.

4. Save your edits once satisfied. **Example**:

5. Before: A travel photo with washed-out skies.

6. After: Enhanced saturation for vivid blue skies and lush greenery.

Advanced RAW Editing Tools

The Galaxy S25 Ultra's RAW image editor (available via One UI 7) offers advanced controls for professional-grade edits:

Key Features of RAW Editor:

1. Adjust exposure, contrast, saturation, vigor, color temperature, and noise levels.

2. Use the histogram to visualize changes in light distribution across your image. **Step-by-Step Tutorial for RAW Editing**:

3. Open a RAW image in Samsung's Expert RAW app.

4. Tap on specific adjustment menus (e.g., Exposure or Saturation).

5. Use sliders to refine each setting while monitoring changes in the histogram.

6. Save edits in JPEG or PNG format for sharing or archiving.

Saving Photos in Different Formats

The Galaxy S25 Ultra allows users to save edited images in various formats depending on their needs:

How to Save Edited Photos:

1. After editing a photo, tap **Save As** from the options menu.

2. Choose between formats like JPEG (optimized for sharing) or PNG (ideal for lossless quality).

3. Select your preferred resolution if prompted (e.g., high-resolution for printing).

Editing Apps Recommendations

While built-in tools are robust, third-party apps provide additional creative freedom and advanced features:

Recommended Apps

1. **Adobe Lightroom Mobile**:

   o Advanced color grading and tone adjustments for professional edits.

   o Example: Edit RAW landscape shots with precise exposure control.

2. **Snapseed**:

   o Free app offering powerful tools like selective adjustments and healing brushes.

   o Example: Remove blemishes from portraits or enhance specific areas of a photo.

3. **Canva**:

   o Ideal for creating graphics or adding text overlays to photos for social media posts.

   o Example: Design Instagram posts with stylish fonts and layouts.

Practical Examples of Editing Techniques

Feature	Before Editing	After Editing
Cropping	Distracting elements around subject	Focused composition
Brightness/Contrast	Dim lighting with flat tones	Balanced exposure with depth
Color Enhancement	Muted colors	Vibrant hues
RAW Adjustments	Overexposed highlights	Recovered details with balanced tones

By mastering these editing tools and techniques on your Galaxy S25 Ultra — whether using built-in features or third-party apps — you'll be able to transform ordinary photos into professional-quality masterpieces!

Best Third-Party Apps for Professional Editing: Reviews and Recommendations

This section provides an in-depth review of popular third-party photo editing apps, highlighting their unique features, strengths, and ideal use cases. Whether you're a beginner or a seasoned photographer, these apps offer tools to elevate your editing game.

1. Adobe Lightroom Mobile
Overview:
Adobe Lightroom Mobile is a powerful app designed for professional-grade photo editing. It supports RAW image editing, offers AI-powered presets, and includes advanced tools like tone curves and selective adjustments.

Key Features:
- **RAW Editing**: Fine-tune exposure, white balance, and colors with precision.
- **AI-Powered Presets**: Automatically enhance portraits, skies, and other elements with adaptive presets.
- **Cloud Integration**: Sync edits across devices for seamless workflow.

Best For:
- Professional photographers or serious hobbyists who need detailed control over their edits.
- Users who work with RAW files regularly.

Recommendation:
Ideal for users comfortable with advanced editing tools who want to achieve professional-quality results.

2. Snapseed
Overview:

Snapseed is a free app by Google that offers a comprehensive suite of editing tools. It's perfect for photographers who want detailed control without paying for premium subscriptions.

Key Features:

- **Selective Adjustments**: Apply edits to specific parts of an image using brushes or masking.
- **Non-Destructive Editing**: Use "Stacks" to adjust or remove edits at any time.
- **Creative Filters**: Includes options like Lens Blur, Retrolux, and Double Exposure for artistic effects.

Best For:

- Intermediate to advanced users who want precise control over their edits.
- Photographers looking for a free yet powerful editing solution.

Recommendation:

Great for detail-oriented photographers who enjoy experimenting with advanced tools.

3. VSCO

Overview:

VSCO combines photo editing with social sharing. It's known for its high-quality filters that emulate film aesthetics and its user-friendly interface.

Key Features:

- **Film-Inspired Filters**: Apply subtle, professional-grade filters to achieve specific moods.
- **Basic Editing Tools**: Adjust exposure, contrast, and saturation with ease.
- **Social Community**: Share your edits within the VSCO community to gain inspiration from other creators.

Best For:

- Beginners who want quick edits with minimal effort.
- Creators focused on achieving a consistent aesthetic for social media platforms like Instagram.

Recommendation:

Perfect for users looking to maintain a cohesive style across their photos without diving into complex adjustments.

4. PicsArt

Overview:

PicsArt is an all-in-one creative platform offering photo editing, collage creation, and graphic design tools. It's ideal for casual users who enjoy adding artistic touches to their photos.

Key Features:

- **AI Effects and Filters**: Transform images with fun effects like cartoon or sketch styles.
- **Text Overlays and Stickers**: Add captions, graphics, or stickers to personalize your photos.
- **Collage Maker**: Combine multiple images into customizable layouts.

Best For:

- Social media enthusiasts who want fun and creative edits.
- Users looking to add text or graphic elements to their photos.

Recommendation:

A great choice for casual photographers or influencers creating content for platforms like TikTok or Pinterest.

5. Polarr

Overview:

Polarr is a versatile app offering both standard editing tools and advanced features like LUT support and tone curve adjustments. Its community-driven approach allows users to create and share custom filters.

Key Features:
- **Custom Filters**: Design your own filters or use those shared by the Polarr community.
- **Advanced Tools**: Includes tone curves, gradient overlays, and RAW support.
- **Cross-Platform Availability**: Works on mobile devices, desktops, and the web.

Best For:
- Advanced users who want full control over their edits.
- Creators interested in experimenting with custom filters and overlays.

Recommendation:

Ideal for photographers who want flexibility across multiple platforms while exploring creative possibilities.

Comparison Table of Recommended Apps

App	Key Features	Best For	Platforms
Adobe Lightroom Mobile	RAW editing, AI presets, cloud sync	Professionals & serious hobbyists	Android, iOS
Snapseed	Selective adjustments, non-destructive edits	Intermediate & advanced photographers	Android, iOS

App	Key Features	Best For	Platforms
VSCO	Film-inspired filters, social sharing	Beginners & social media creators	Android, iOS
PicsArt	AI effects, stickers, collage maker	Casual users & influencers	Android, iOS
Polarr	Custom filters, tone curves	Advanced users & experimental creators	Android, iOS

Recommended Apps Based on Skill Levels

1. **Beginners**:
   o Start with VSCO or PicsArt for quick edits and easy-to-use interfaces.
   o Use built-in presets to achieve polished results without extensive knowledge of editing techniques.
2. **Intermediate Users**:
   o Experiment with Snapseed's selective adjustments and creative filters.
   o Try Polarr for more control over gradients and overlays while exploring custom filters.
3. **Advanced Users/Professionals**:
   o Leverage Adobe Lightroom Mobile's RAW editing capabilities for precise adjustments.
   o Use Polarr's LUT support and tone curves for cinematic effects in your photos.

By choosing the right third-party app based on your skill level and needs, you can unlock the full potential of your Galaxy S25 Ultra's photography capabilities while creating stunning visuals tailored to your style!

AI-Powered Enhancements for Quick Edits: Before-and-After Examples

AI-powered photo editing tools have revolutionized how we enhance and refine images, making professional-level edits accessible to everyone. These tools automatically adjust exposure, contrast, colors, and more, saving time while delivering impressive results. Below, we explore how AI works, provide examples of its impact, and discuss its capabilities for removing noise, fixing overexposure, and enhancing portraits.

How AI-Powered Tools Enhance Photos

AI-powered tools use machine learning algorithms to analyze images and apply intelligent adjustments. These tools can:

- Automatically balance exposure and contrast.
- Enhance color vibrancy and saturation.
- Remove noise and sharpen details.
- Restore overexposed or underexposed areas.
- Retouch portraits while preserving natural features.

Before-and-After Examples of AI Enhancements

1. Exposure and Contrast Adjustment

AI tools can fix uneven lighting by brightening shadows and reducing highlights for a balanced look.

- **Before**: A landscape photo with overexposed skies and dark foreground details.
- **After**: The AI tool adjusts the exposure to reveal details in the sky while brightening the shadows in the foreground.

2. Color Enhancement

AI enhances color vibrancy to make photos more visually appealing without oversaturation.

- **Before**: A food photo with dull colors under dim lighting.
- **After**: AI boosts saturation and contrast, making the dish look vibrant and appetizing.

3. Noise Reduction

High ISO settings or low-light conditions often introduce noise (graininess) into photos. AI tools can eliminate noise while retaining details.

- **Before**: A nighttime cityscape with visible grain in the sky.
- **After**: The AI removes noise, resulting in a cleaner image with sharper edges.

4. Portrait Retouching

AI-powered portrait enhancers refine skin tones, reduce blemishes, and adjust lighting for professional-quality results.

- **Before**: A portrait with uneven lighting and visible imperfections.
- **After**: The AI smooths skin textures, balances highlights/shadows, and enhances facial features while maintaining a natural look.

How to Use AI Tools for Specific Enhancements

1. Removing Noise

Noise reduction is essential for improving image clarity in low-light or high ISO photos.

- Use tools like Topaz Photo AI or Adobe Lightroom's Noise Reduction feature to clean up grainy images.
- Example: A photo of a starry night sky is enhanced by reducing noise while keeping the stars sharp.

2. Fixing Overexposure

Overexposed areas lose detail due to excessive brightness. AI tools can recover these details effectively.

- Use Adobe Photoshop's Neural Filters or BeFunky's Image Enhancer to restore blown-out highlights.
- Example: A beach photo with an overexposed sky is corrected to reveal cloud textures and subtle gradients.

3. Enhancing Portraits

Portrait-specific AI tools refine facial features without making them look artificial.

- Use apps like BeFunky's Portrait Enhancer or Snapseed's Face Enhance tool to retouch skin tones, brighten eyes, or add subtle highlights.
- Example: A selfie taken in poor lighting is transformed into a polished portrait with balanced tones and smooth textures.

Recommended AI Tools for Quick Edits

Tool	Key Features	Best For
Adobe Lightroom Mobile	Noise reduction, color grading, RAW editing	Professional photographers
Topaz Photo AI	Noise removal, sharpening, resolution upscaling	Low-light or blurry photos
BeFunky	One-click enhancements, portrait retouching	Social media-ready images
Snapseed	Selective adjustments, face retouching	Creative edits with precise control
Vance AI	Pixel repair, color enhancement	Old or pixelated images

How to Get Started with AI Editing

1. **Choose Your Tool**:

    o For quick edits: Use BeFunky or Snapseed.

    o For advanced control: Opt for Adobe Lightroom Mobile or Topaz Photo AI.

2. **Upload Your Image**:

    o Open your chosen app and upload the photo you want to edit.

3. **Apply Enhancements**:

- o Use one-click enhancement options for quick fixes or manually tweak settings like exposure and contrast for finer control.

4. **Save Your Work**:

- o Export your edited image in high resolution (JPEG or PNG) for sharing or printing.

Practical Examples of Before-and-After Scenarios

Scenario	Before	After
Landscape Photo	Overexposed sky; dark foreground	Balanced exposure; vibrant colors
Food Photography	Dull colors under dim lighting	Enhanced saturation; appetizing look
Nighttime Cityscape	Grainy image with noise	Clean image with sharp details
Portrait	Uneven skin tones; poor lighting	Smooth skin; balanced highlights

AI-powered enhancements allow you to transform ordinary photos into professional-quality visuals effortlessly. Whether you're fixing exposure issues, reducing noise, or enhancing portraits, these tools save time while delivering stunning results. By leveraging apps like Adobe Lightroom Mobile, Snapseed, or BeFunky alongside your Galaxy S25 Ultra's powerful camera capabilities, you can elevate your photography game with ease!

Chapter 8: Low-Light and Night Photography Mastery

Perfecting Night Mode Settings for Astrophotography: Tips and Tricks

The Samsung Galaxy S25 Ultra is a powerhouse for low-light and night photography, thanks to its advanced Night Mode, Astro Mode, and AI-powered enhancements. Whether you're capturing the starry sky or vibrant cityscapes, understanding how to optimize these features will help you achieve stunning results. This section focuses on mastering Night Mode for astrophotography, providing practical tips on exposure, noise reduction, and long-exposure techniques.

Using Night Mode for Astrophotography

Night Mode on the Galaxy S25 Ultra utilizes extended exposure times and AI processing to brighten dark scenes while preserving details. It's perfect for capturing stars, constellations, or cityscapes at night.

How to Use Night Mode:

1. Open the **Camera app**.

2. Swipe to **More** and select **Night Mode**.

3. Frame your shot and hold the phone steady (or use a tripod).

4. Tap the shutter button and wait for the progress bar to complete before moving your phone.

5. Let the AI process the image for optimal brightness and clarity.

Pro Tip:

6. Use a tripod or place your phone on a stable surface to minimize motion blur during long exposures.

7. Avoid bright artificial lights in the frame, as they can cause lens flares.

Adjusting Exposure and Long-Exposure Settings

For astrophotography or detailed night shots, adjusting exposure settings manually can significantly enhance your photos.

Tips for Adjusting Exposure:

1. **Enable Pro Mode**:
   - Open the Camera app, swipe to **More**, and select **Pro Mode**.
   - Manually adjust the shutter speed (up to 30 seconds) for long exposures.
2. **Set ISO Levels**:
   - Use lower ISO settings (e.g., ISO 100–400) to reduce noise in well-lit areas.
   - Increase ISO (e.g., ISO 800–1600) for darker environments but monitor noise levels.
3. **Use Astro Mode**:
   - Access Astro Mode via Expert RAW in the Camera app.
   - Set exposure times between 4–10 minutes for capturing star trails or constellations.

Pro Tip:

4. Use a remote shutter or timer function to avoid shaking the phone when pressing the shutter button.
5. For starry skies, find locations with minimal light pollution for clearer results.

Reducing Noise and Enhancing Details

Low-light conditions often introduce noise into photos, but the Galaxy S25 Ultra's AI-powered tools make it easy to reduce noise while retaining sharp details.

Noise Reduction Techniques:

1. Enable AI Scene Optimization:

   o Go to Camera settings > Enable Scene Optimizer.

   o The AI will automatically detect low-light conditions and enhance brightness while reducing noise.

2. Use Super HDR:

   o HDR balances highlights and shadows, ensuring well-lit areas don't overexpose while enhancing darker regions.

Pro Tip:

3. For astrophotography, enable Adaptive Pixel technology in Pro Mode to merge multiple exposures into one clear image.

4. Post-process images using third-party apps like Adobe Lightroom Mobile or Snapseed for advanced noise reduction and sharpening.

Practical Examples

Scenario	Technique Used	Result
Starry Sky	Astro Mode with 10-minute exposure	Clear constellations with sharp stars
Cityscape at Night	Night Mode + Super HDR	Brightened streets with reduced glare
Milky Way Photography	Pro Mode with long exposure (30 seconds)	Vibrant Milky Way with minimal noise

Common Issues and Solutions

1. **Banding in Night Photos**:
   Some users reported banding issues in early software versions of the Galaxy S25 Ultra's Night Mode. Ensure your phone is updated by navigating to:
   Settings > Software Update > Download and Install.
   This update resolves post-processing glitches affecting night photos.

2. **Soft Details in Astro Shots**:
   - Use a tripod to eliminate shake during long exposures.
   - Avoid windy conditions that can cause slight vibrations in your setup.

The Samsung Galaxy S25 Ultra's advanced Night Mode features make it easier than ever to capture stunning astrophotography and low-light scenes. By combining tools like Astro Mode, Pro Mode, and AI Scene Optimization with proper techniques such as using a tripod and adjusting exposure settings, you can create professional-grade night photos that truly stand out. Whether photographing stars or vibrant cityscapes, mastering these features will take your photography skills to new heights!

Capturing Light Trails and Neon Shots Like a Pro: Step-by-Step Guide

The Samsung Galaxy S25 Ultra's advanced camera capabilities make it ideal for capturing stunning light trails and neon shots. These techniques rely on long exposures, precise settings, and creative compositions to transform ordinary night scenes into mesmerizing visuals. This section provides step-by-step instructions for achieving professional-quality results.

Capturing Light Trails

Light trails are created by recording the movement of light sources (e.g., car headlights or fireworks) over time using long exposure photography. Here's how to master this technique:

Step-by-Step Guide for Light Trails

1. **Choose the Right Location**:
    - o Find a spot with moving lights, such as busy roads, bridges, or roundabouts. Elevated vantage points like rooftops or hills can add perspective.
2. **Set Up Your Camera**:
    - o Use a tripod to stabilize your phone and prevent motion blur during long exposures.
    - o Enable **Pro Mode** or **Night Mode** on your Galaxy S25 Ultra.
3. **Adjust Camera Settings**:
    - o **Shutter Speed**: Set it between 10–30 seconds to capture long light trails. For ultra-long exposures, use Bulb mode.
    - o **ISO**: Keep ISO low (e.g., ISO 100–200) to reduce noise and avoid overexposure.
    - o **Aperture**: Use an aperture between f/5 and f/11 for balanced brightness.
4. **Compose Your Shot**:
    - o Leave enough room in the frame for the light trails to flow naturally.
    - o Include foreground elements like railings or trees to add depth and context.
5. **Capture the Shot**:
    - o Press the shutter button and let the camera record the scene.

- o Experiment with different angles and exposure times for varied effects.

Example:

- **Before**: A photo of a city street at night with static car lights.
- **After**: Long exposure reveals vibrant streaks of red and white light weaving through the frame.

Capturing Neon Shots

Neon signs are perfect subjects for night photography due to their vivid colors and glowing effects. Here's how to make them stand out:

Step-by-Step Guide for Neon Photography

1. **Find Neon Signs**:
   - o Look for brightly lit storefronts, billboards, or street signs in urban areas.
2. **Set Up Your Camera**:
   - o Use a tripod or steady surface to avoid camera shake.

- o Enable Pro Mode for manual control.
3. **Adjust Camera Settings**:
    - o **Shutter Speed**: Use shorter exposures (e.g., 1–5 seconds) to prevent overexposure of neon lights.
    - o **ISO**: Set ISO between 200–400 for balanced brightness without noise.
    - o **White Balance**: Adjust white balance manually to emphasize the neon's colors (e.g., cooler tones for blue signs, warmer tones for red signs).
4. **Compose Your Shot**:
    - o Frame the neon sign creatively by including reflections in puddles or glass surfaces.
    - o Focus on symmetry or isolate specific letters or shapes.
5. **Capture the Shot**:
    - o Tap to focus on the brightest part of the neon sign.
    - o Experiment with angles, such as shooting from below for dramatic effects.

Example:
- **Before**: A dimly lit photo of a neon sign with uneven brightness.
- **After**: Enhanced colors and sharp details highlight the glow of the sign.

Tips for Success

Light Trails:
- Shoot during twilight or early evening when ambient light adds atmosphere without overpowering trails.
- Use ND filters if ambient light is too bright; this allows longer exposures without overexposing highlights.

Neon Shots:

- Include reflections in windows or puddles to add depth and interest.
- Avoid direct light sources near neon signs that might create glare or lens flares.

Practical Examples

Scenario	Technique Used	Result
Light Trails on Roads	Long exposure (30 seconds) + low ISO	Vibrant streaks of car headlights
Roundabout Light Trails	Elevated vantage point + wide aperture	Circular patterns of flowing light
Neon Sign Close-Up	Short exposure + manual white balance	Sharp details with glowing colors

By mastering long exposure techniques and leveraging manual settings on your Galaxy S25 Ultra, you can create captivating light trail and neon shots that showcase your creativity. Whether you're photographing bustling city streets or glowing storefronts, these tips will help you achieve professional-quality results!

Noise Reduction Techniques for Crisp Low-Light Portraits: Practical Advice

Low-light portraits often suffer from digital noise, which can diminish the quality of the image by introducing graininess and false colors. The Samsung Galaxy S25 Ultra, equipped with advanced features like RAW shooting and AI-powered enhancements, provides tools to tackle noise effectively. This section explores techniques for reducing noise in low-light portraits, including camera settings, post-processing workflows, and practical positioning strategies.

Understanding Noise in Low-Light Portraits

Noise typically appears as grainy textures or colored speckles in digital images, especially when using high ISO settings or underexposed shots. It is more prominent in shadows or darker areas due to limited light data reaching the sensor. Reducing noise while preserving details requires careful balance during both shooting and editing.

Techniques for Reducing Noise

1. Shooting in RAW

- RAW files retain all image data from the sensor, allowing more flexibility when reducing noise during post-processing.

- Use the Galaxy S25 Ultra's **Expert RAW mode** to capture portraits with maximum detail retention.

- Example: A portrait shot in RAW at ISO 800 can be processed later to reduce noise without sacrificing sharpness.

2. Adjusting Camera Settings

Proper camera settings can minimize noise during shooting:

- **ISO**: Use the lowest possible ISO setting (e.g., ISO 100–400) to reduce noise while maintaining adequate exposure.

- **Shutter Speed**: Pair a slower shutter speed with a tripod to allow more light into the sensor without increasing ISO.

- **Aperture**: Use a wide aperture (e.g., f/1.8–f/2.8) to let in more light and reduce reliance on high ISO.

3. Using AI Noise Reduction Tools

The Galaxy S25 Ultra's built-in AI Scene Optimizer automatically reduces noise by analyzing the image and applying intelligent corrections.

- Enable **Scene Optimizer** in camera settings for low-light conditions.

- Example: A dimly lit portrait with visible grain is transformed into a smoother image with enhanced details.

Positioning Subjects Near Light Sources

Strategic placement of your subject can significantly improve lighting and reduce noise:

1. **Use Natural Light**:

   o Position your subject near windows or open doors where soft natural light is available.

   o Example: A portrait taken near a window during twilight minimizes shadows and reduces noise.

2. **Artificial Light Sources**:

   o Use lamps or LED panels to illuminate your subject evenly without harsh shadows.

- o Example: A desk lamp angled toward the subject creates soft highlights that brighten the image.

3. **Reflectors**:

   - o Use white reflectors or even a piece of white cardboard to bounce light onto your subject's face, reducing shadow-induced noise.

   - o Example: A reflector positioned opposite a light source fills in shadows under the chin.

Post-Processing for Noise Reduction

Editing tools can further refine low-light portraits by removing residual noise while preserving details:

1. Adobe Lightroom Mobile

- Adjust sliders like **Luminance Noise Reduction** to smooth grainy textures while retaining sharpness.

- Fine-tune **Luminance Detail** and **Contrast** sliders for balanced results.

2. Topaz DeNoise AI

- Use AI algorithms to target specific areas of the image for advanced noise reduction without losing fine details.

3. Snapseed

- Apply selective adjustments to reduce noise only in shadowed areas while keeping brighter regions untouched.

Before-and-After Examples

Scenario	Before	After
Dimly Lit Portrait	Grainy textures on skin; muted colors	Smooth skin tones; vibrant colors
Shadowed Background	Noise visible in dark areas	Clean background with sharp edges
High ISO Night Portrait	False color speckles; loss of detail	Reduced grain; preserved facial details

Practical Tips for Success

1. **Use Long Exposure Noise Reduction**:

   o   Enable this feature on the Galaxy S25 Ultra for cleaner results during long exposures.

2. **Avoid Overprocessing**:

   o   Excessive noise reduction can result in overly smooth images that lose natural texture.

3. **Test Multiple Light Sources**:

   o   Experiment with different lighting setups (e.g., softbox vs LED panel) to find optimal illumination for your subject.

By combining proper camera settings, strategic positioning near light sources, and advanced post-processing techniques, you can achieve crisp, professional-quality low-light portraits with minimal noise using your Galaxy S25 Ultra!

Chapter 9: Smart AI Features - Redefining Mobile Photography

AI Scene Optimization for Perfect Shots Every Time: How It Works

Artificial Intelligence (AI) has transformed mobile photography, making it more intuitive and accessible. One of the most impactful advancements is **AI Scene Optimization**, which automatically adjusts camera settings based on the scene being captured. This feature simplifies the photography process while delivering professional-quality results. Below, we explore how AI Scene Optimization works, its benefits, and practical tips for using it effectively.

How AI Scene Optimization Works

AI Scene Optimization uses machine learning algorithms to analyze elements in a scene—such as lighting, colors, objects, and textures—and adjusts camera settings accordingly. The AI categorizes the scene (e.g., landscape, portrait, food) and fine-tunes parameters like exposure, white balance, contrast, and saturation to enhance image quality.

Key Features of AI Scene Optimization:

1. **Scene Detection**:

   o AI identifies the type of scene in real-time (e.g., sunset, portrait, or cityscape).

   o Example: It detects a landscape and boosts vibrancy for lush greens and vivid skies.

2. **Object Recognition**:

   o Recognizes objects within the frame (e.g., faces, animals, or buildings) and optimizes focus and lighting.

   o Example: It highlights facial features in portraits while softening the background.

3. **Dynamic Adjustments**:

   o Automatically balances exposure in high-contrast scenes to retain details in both highlights and shadows.

   o Example: It brightens foreground subjects while maintaining the dramatic colors of a sunset.

4. **Continuous Learning**:

   o AI improves its accuracy over time by learning from vast datasets of images and user feedback.

Benefits of AI Scene Optimization

AI Scene Optimization enhances photo quality by intelligently adjusting key settings without requiring manual intervention. This feature is particularly useful for both novice photographers and professionals looking for quick edits.

How It Enhances Photo Quality:

- **Optimized Exposure**: Prevents overexposure or underexposure by balancing light levels across the frame.

- **Enhanced Contrast**: Adds depth to images by refining shadows and highlights.

- **Vivid Colors**: Boosts saturation and vibrancy to make photos visually striking.

- **Reduced Noise**: Applies noise reduction algorithms in low-light conditions for cleaner images.

Example Scenarios:

1. **Landscape Photography**:

   o Before: A dull photo with muted greens and an overexposed sky.

   o After: AI enhances vibrancy, balances exposure, and adds contrast for a dramatic effect.

2. **Portrait Photography**:

   o Before: Uneven lighting on a subject's face with distracting background elements.

   o After: AI brightens skin tones, softens the background, and sharpens facial details.

Tips for Using AI Scene Optimization Effectively

1. Activate AI Scene Optimization

- Enable the feature in your Galaxy S25 Ultra's camera settings by toggling "Scene Optimizer."

- Point your camera at the subject; the AI will automatically detect the scene type.

2. Pair with Manual Adjustments

- While AI handles most settings automatically, you can fine-tune parameters like brightness or saturation in Pro Mode for added control.

3. Experiment with Different Scenes

- Use AI optimization for diverse scenarios such as food photography (enhanced textures), landscapes (vivid colors), or portraits (balanced skin tones).

4. Leverage Low-Light Capabilities

- Combine AI optimization with Night Mode to capture sharp details in dim environments while reducing noise.

Before-and-After Examples

Scenario	Before	After
Landscape Photography	Muted greens; overexposed sky	Vibrant greens; balanced sky tones
Food Photography	Dull colors; uneven lighting	Enhanced textures; vibrant hues
Portrait Photography	Shadows on face; harsh background	Brightened skin tones; softened background

Practical Applications of AI Scene Optimization

1. **Travel Photography**:

   o Capture vibrant landscapes or architectural details effortlessly.

o   Example: A photo of a mountain range becomes sharper with enhanced greens and blues.

2. **Social Media Content Creation**:

   o   Use optimized shots for Instagram or TikTok posts that stand out with vivid colors and balanced compositions.

   o   Example: A food photo gains rich textures that make it visually appealing.

3. **Low-Light Portraits**:

   o   Combine AI optimization with Night Mode to reduce noise while retaining sharp facial details.

   o   Example: A selfie taken at dusk appears brighter with natural-looking skin tones.

AI Scene Optimization redefines mobile photography by making it smarter and more accessible. Whether you're capturing landscapes, portraits, or low-light scenes, this feature ensures perfect shots every time by automating complex adjustments like exposure, contrast, and color balance. By leveraging this technology on your Galaxy S25 Ultra alongside manual tweaks when needed, you can elevate your photography to professional levels effortlessly!

Object Eraser and Background Blur Explained: Examples and Use Cases

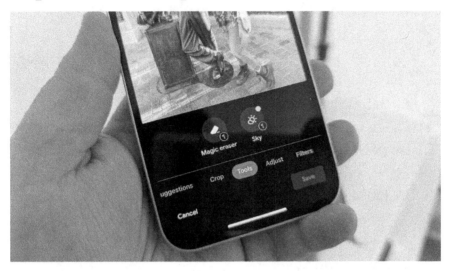

The Samsung Galaxy S25 Ultra offers advanced tools like the **Object Eraser** and **Background Blur (Bokeh)** to enhance photo quality and focus on the subject. These features are particularly useful for removing distractions and creating professional-looking portraits. Below is a detailed guide on how these tools work, their use cases, and examples of their impact.

Object Eraser: Removing Unwanted Objects

The Object Eraser tool uses AI technology to seamlessly remove unwanted objects, people, or distractions from photos by analyzing the surrounding area and filling in the gaps. This feature is perfect for cleaning up cluttered images or refining compositions.

How to Use the Object Eraser

1. **Access the Tool**:
   - Open your photo in the Galaxy S25 Ultra's gallery app.
   - Tap the **Edit** icon and select the **Magic Eraser** tool.
2. **Select the Object**:
   - Adjust the brush size using the slider.
   - Paint over the object you want to remove, ensuring full coverage.
3. **Erase**:
   - Tap **Erase Object**, and the AI will remove it while blending the background seamlessly.
4. **Apply and Save**:
   - Once satisfied, click **Apply** to finalize your edits.

Examples of Object/Magic Eraser in Action

- **Before**: A travel photo with a distracting photobomber in the background.
- **After**: The photobomber is removed, leaving a clean and scenic view.
- **Before**: A food photo with crumbs or stray utensils cluttering the frame.
- **After**: The crumbs are erased, highlighting the dish's presentation.

Use Cases for Object Eraser

1. **Portrait Photography**:
   - Remove distracting elements like stray objects or other people in group shots.
2. **Travel Photography**:
   - Eliminate unwanted tourists from iconic landmarks for cleaner compositions.
3. **Product Photography**:
   - Remove clutter or imperfections to focus solely on the product.

Background Blur (Bokeh): Creating Depth

Background Blur (Bokeh) uses depth sensors to isolate the subject from its surroundings, applying a smooth blur effect to the background. This technique enhances portraits by drawing attention to the subject while softening distractions.

How Background Blur Works

1. **Activate Portrait Mode**:
   - Open the camera app and select "Portrait Mode."
2. **Adjust Blur Intensity**:
   - Use the slider to control how much blur is applied to the background.
3. **Focus on Your Subject**:
   - Tap on your subject to ensure sharp focus while blurring everything else.
4. **Capture Your Shot**:
   - Take your photo and preview results with real-time adjustments.
5. **How to Apply Background Blur to Photos**
   - Start by opening the Gallery app, then select the photo you want to edit.
   - Swipe up on the photo and tap on the "Background Blur" option.
   - The phone will automatically analyze the photo and apply a background blur; users can adjust the blur intensity from 0 (none) to 7 (maximum).
   - Once satisfied, tap "Save" to finalize the edit; viewers are encouraged to subscribe for more tech tutorials.

Examples of Background Blur in Action

- **Before**: A portrait with a busy background featuring cars and buildings.

- **After**: The background is blurred, emphasizing facial details while eliminating distractions.
- **Before**: A candid photo with uneven lighting in a crowded space.
- **After**: The subject stands out against a soft, blurred backdrop.

Use Cases for Background Blur

1. **Portraits**:
   - Highlight facial features while creating a professional studio-like effect.
2. **Event Photography**:
   - Focus on key subjects during weddings or parties while minimizing background chaos.
3. **Creative Shots**:
   - Add artistic flair by blurring colorful lights or patterns behind your subject.

Practical Scenarios Where These Features Shine

Scenario	Feature Used	Result
Travel Photo	Object Eraser	Removes tourists from iconic landmarks
Food Photography	Object Eraser	Cleans up stray crumbs or utensils
Portrait in Busy Street	Background Blur	Highlights subject against blurred cars
Wedding Portrait	Background Blur	Softens crowd noise for elegant focus

The Object Eraser and Background Blur tools redefine mobile photography by offering advanced editing capabilities directly on your Galaxy S25 Ultra. Whether you're removing distractions from portraits or creating depth with bokeh effects, these features are invaluable for producing clean, professional-quality images tailored to your creative vision!

Live Focus vs. Portrait Mode Comparison: When to Use Each

The Samsung Galaxy S25 Ultra offers **Portrait Mode**, which incorporates and expands upon the features of the older **Live Focus** mode. While both modes are designed to create stunning portraits with background blur (bokeh), they differ in terms of functionality, effects, and use cases. This section compares the two modes, explains their differences, and provides practical advice on when to use each for optimal results.

Key Differences Between Live Focus and Portrait Mode

Feature	Live Focus	Portrait Mode
Availability	Found on older Galaxy devices (pre-One UI 4)	Available on newer Galaxy devices (One UI 4+)
Background Effects	Basic blur adjustment	Advanced effects like Studio, Color Point, etc.
Video Capability	Limited to photos	Supports both photos and videos

Feature	Live Focus	Portrait Mode
Control Over Bokeh	Adjustable blur intensity	More control with additional filters

Live Focus: Overview and Use Cases

Live Focus is a feature from earlier Galaxy devices that allows users to blur the background of an image while keeping the subject in sharp focus. It offers basic bokeh effects and is ideal for quick portrait shots.

When to Use Live Focus

1. **Quick Portraits**:
   - If you need a simple background blur without additional effects.
   - Example: A quick headshot with a softly blurred background.
2. **Limited Lighting Conditions**:

- o Works well in evenly lit environments where subject-background separation is clear.

3. **Minimal Editing Needs**:
   - o Ideal for users who don't require advanced post-capture editing.

Example:
- A photo of a friend at a café with the background blurred to remove distractions.

Portrait Mode: Overview and Use Cases

Portrait Mode replaces Live Focus on newer Galaxy devices and offers enhanced functionality, including advanced filters, better edge detection, and support for video recording. It uses AI and depth sensors to deliver professional-quality results.

Key Features of Portrait Mode

1. **Advanced Background Effects**:
   - o Offers effects like Blur, Studio, High-Key Mono, Low-Key Mono, Backdrop, and Color Point.
   - o Example: Use the Color Point effect to keep the subject in color while desaturating the background.

2. **Portrait Video**:
   - o Allows users to apply bokeh effects while recording video.
   - o Example: Record a vlog with a blurred background to keep the focus on you.

3. **Post-Capture Editing**:

- Adjust background effects or blur intensity after taking the photo.

When to Use Portrait Mode

1. **Creative Portraits**:

    - Perfect for adding artistic flair with advanced effects like Studio or Backdrop.

    - Example: A black-and-white portrait using High-Key Mono for dramatic impact.

2. **Portrait Videos**:

    - Use for creating cinematic videos with blurred backgrounds.

3. **Challenging Backgrounds**:

    - Handles complex backgrounds better due to improved AI processing.

Example:

- A professional portrait with Studio lighting applied to brighten the subject while keeping the background neutral.

Practical Tips for Using Each Mode

Tips for Live Focus

- Ensure good lighting and clear subject-background separation for best results.

- Avoid using Live Focus in low-light conditions as it may struggle with edge detection.

Tips for Portrait Mode

1. Experiment with Filters:

   o Try different effects like Color Point or Backdrop for creative results.

2. Adjust Blur Intensity:

   o Use the slider in Portrait Mode to control how much blur is applied.

3. Use Sufficient Lighting:

   o Portrait Mode works best in well-lit environments but can handle slightly dimmer conditions compared to Live Focus.

Before-and-After Examples

Scenario	Before	After
Simple Portrait (Live Focus)	Busy café background	Subject stands out with soft bokeh
Creative Portrait (Portrait Mode)	Flat lighting; no depth	Studio effect brightens subject; dramatic backdrop
Portrait Video	Background cluttered	Smooth bokeh keeps focus on subject

While Live Focus is great for quick and simple portraits, Portrait Mode offers more versatility and creative control with advanced filters and video capabilities. For casual shots, Live Focus may suffice, but if you're looking to elevate your photography or videography with artistic effects and precise adjustments, Portrait Mode is the go-to option. By understanding when to use each mode, you can make the most of your Galaxy S25 Ultra's powerful camera system!

Chapter 10: Troubleshooting & Optimizing Performance

Fixing Common Camera Issues (Blurry Photos, Lag): Troubleshooting Guide

The Samsung Galaxy S25 Ultra is equipped with advanced camera features, but like any device, it can encounter issues such as blurry photos or camera lag. This chapter provides a comprehensive guide to troubleshooting these common problems, ensuring you can optimize your device for the best possible performance.

Common Camera Issues and Solutions

1. **Blurry Photos**

   o **Causes**: Camera shake, incorrect focus, dirty lenses, or low light conditions.

   o **Troubleshooting Steps**:

      1. **Use a Tripod**: Stabilize your camera to prevent motion blur.

      2. **Clean the Lens**: Ensure the camera lens is free from smudges or debris.

      3. **Check Focus**: Tap on the screen to focus on your subject.

      4. **Adjust Settings**: Use **Super Steady mode** for smoother video or **Night Mode** for low-light conditions.

- o **Prevention Tip**: Use a remote shutter or timer to avoid camera shake.

2. **Camera Lag**

   - o **Causes**: Insufficient storage, outdated software, or too many apps running in the background.

   - o **Troubleshooting Steps**:

     1. **Free Up Storage**: Delete unused photos or apps to ensure ample storage space.

     2. **Update Software**: Ensure your device and camera app are updated to the latest version.

     3. **Close Background Apps**: Minimize apps running in the background to free up resources.

   - o **Prevention Tip**: Regularly clean up storage and update your device to maintain performance.

3. **Overheating During Video Recording**

   - o **Causes**: Extended recording sessions, high ambient temperatures, or resource-intensive settings.

   - o **Troubleshooting Steps**:

     1. **Take Breaks**: Pause recording periodically to cool down the device.

     2. **Adjust Settings**: Lower resolution or frame rate to reduce processing demands.

3. **Use External Cooling**: Consider using a phone cooler or recording in a cooler environment.

o **Prevention Tip**: Record in well-ventilated areas and avoid prolonged sessions.

Optimizing Camera Performance

1. Regular Maintenance

- **Clean the Lens**: Use a soft cloth to wipe away smudges or fingerprints.

- **Update Camera App**: Ensure you have the latest camera software for bug fixes and feature enhancements.

2. Optimize Storage

- **Free Up Space**: Regularly delete unused photos or transfer them to external storage.

- **Use Cloud Services**: Consider using cloud storage like Google Photos to free up local space.

3. Improve Focus

- **Use Tap-to-Focus**: Tap on your subject to ensure sharp focus.

- **Enable AF/AE Lock**: Lock focus and exposure on your subject for consistent results.

Tips for Preventing Issues in the Future

1. **Use a Tripod or Stabilizer**:

- For video recording or low-light conditions to prevent camera shake.
2. **Regularly Update Software**:
   - Stay updated with the latest patches and features to avoid compatibility issues.
3. **Monitor Storage**:
   - Keep enough free space to prevent lag or crashes during photo sessions.
4. **Use Protective Cases**:
   - Protect your device from physical damage that could affect camera performance.

Before-and-After Examples

Issue	Before	After
Blurry Photos	Unstable camera; blurry image	Sharp image with tripod stabilization
Camera Lag	Slow app response; delayed shutter	Smooth performance after software update
Overheating	Device overheats during recording	Normal temperature with breaks and cooling

Storage Management Tips for Heavy Shooters: Best Practices

Managing storage effectively is crucial for photographers and videographers who generate large volumes of digital files. Whether you're capturing high-resolution images or shooting 4K videos, implementing strategies to free up space, organize files, and back up your data can streamline your workflow and prevent storage-related issues. Below are best practices for managing storage efficiently.

Strategies for Managing Storage

1. Freeing Up Space

- **Delete Unused Files**:

    o Regularly review your photo library to delete duplicates, blurry shots, or files you no longer need.

    o Example: Use built-in tools like Samsung's Gallery Cleaner to identify and remove redundant files.

- **Shrink Large Files**:

    o Flatten TIFF or PSD files after editing to reduce their size without losing essential details.

    o Example: A layered PSD file can be flattened to save significant space while retaining the final edit.

- **Offload Files to External Storage**:

    o Transfer older photos and videos to external SSDs or hard drives to free up device storage.

2. Using Cloud Storage

- **Benefits of Cloud Storage**:

- o Access your files anywhere and ensure redundancy without relying solely on physical drives.

- o Example: Services like Google Photos or Dropbox allow automatic backups and easy sharing.

- **Best Practices**:

  - o Enable automatic uploads for new photos and videos.

  - o Use cloud storage as part of a **3-2-1 backup strategy**, where one copy is stored off-site.

3. Expanding Storage with External Drives

- **External SSDs**:

  - o Invest in high-quality SSDs like Kingston XS2000, which offer fast read/write speeds and capacities up to 4TB.

  - o Example: Use external SSDs for quick access to archived photos during on-the-go editing.

- **RAID Systems**:

  - o For professionals managing terabytes of data, RAID systems provide reliability and protection against drive failures.

  - o Example: A RAID setup can combine multiple drives into a single unit, ensuring redundancy.

Organizing Files Efficiently

1. Categorize by Date or Event

- Create folders labeled by year, month, or event name (e.g., "2025_Travel_Paris") for easy navigation.

- Example: Store all wedding photos from April in a folder named "2025_Wedding_April."

2. Use Metadata Tags

- Add keywords or tags to files (e.g., "landscape," "portrait") for faster searches.

- Example: Tag photos with "sunset" or "beach" for quick retrieval during editing.

3. Implement a File Naming Convention

- Use consistent naming formats that include date and subject (e.g., "2025_04_Paris_Sunset.jpg").

- Example: Rename raw files from "IMG_1234.CR2" to "2025_04_Mountain_Shot.CR2" for clarity.

Recommendations for Heavy Shooters

Strategy	Benefits	Tools/Services
Cloud Storage	Remote access; redundancy	Google Photos, Dropbox
External SSDs	Speed; durability	Kingston XS2000, Samsung T7
RAID Systems	Reliability; large capacity	Synology NAS

Strategy	Benefits	Tools/Services
Metadata Tagging	Easy file retrieval	Adobe Lightroom
File Naming Conventions	Organized archives	Manual or automated renaming tools

By combining regular file cleanup, leveraging external and cloud storage solutions, and organizing your files systematically, heavy shooters can manage their growing photo and video libraries efficiently. These best practices not only optimize storage but also ensure easy access to your creative content whenever needed!

Maintaining Your Camera Lenses for Longevity: Cleaning and Care Tips

Keeping your camera lenses clean and free of smudges is essential for ensuring sharp, high-quality photos and extending the lifespan of your equipment. Dirty lenses can cause blurry images, reduce contrast, and even damage optical coatings over time. This guide provides step-by-step instructions for safely cleaning lenses, tips for protecting them from scratches, and advice on maintaining their condition.

Importance of Clean Lenses

1. **Image Quality**:
   - Dust, smudges, and fingerprints on the lens can degrade image sharpness and contrast.

- o Example: A water droplet or fingerprint can create blurry spots in your photo.

2. **Longevity**:

   - o Regular cleaning prevents buildup of oils or debris that could damage optical coatings over time.

   - o Proper maintenance helps retain the lens's value and ensures it performs optimally for years.

Step-by-Step Instructions for Cleaning Lenses

1. Prepare Your Tools

- **Air Blower**: Removes loose dust without touching the lens surface.
- **Soft-Bristled Brush**: Ideal for removing stubborn particles without scratching the glass.
- **Microfiber Cloth**: Safe for wiping smudges without leaving streaks or residue.
- **Lens Cleaning Solution**: Removes oil and fingerprints effectively; use sparingly.

2. Cleaning Process

1. **Use an Air Blower**:
   - o Hold the lens facing downward to prevent particles from settling back on the surface.
   - o Blow away loose dust and dirt gently.
2. **Brush Off Stubborn Debris**:
   - o Use a soft-bristled brush (e.g., camel or goat hair) to remove particles stuck to the lens.
   - o Avoid touching the brush bristles with oily fingers to prevent smudging.
3. **Wipe with Microfiber Cloth**:

- o Apply a drop or two of lens cleaning solution to the cloth (not directly on the lens).
- o Wipe in small circular motions, starting from the center and moving outward.
- o Avoid scrubbing; gentle pressure is sufficient.

4. **Check Your Work**:
   - o Use a flashlight to inspect for remaining smudges or streaks.
   - o Repeat steps as needed but avoid excessive cleaning to protect optical coatings.

5. **Clean the Lens Exterior**:
   - o Wipe off residues or dirt on the barrel using a dry microfiber cloth.
   - o Example: Dust on zoom rings or focus rings won't affect image quality but contributes to overall maintenance.

6. **Allow Air Drying**:
   - o Let the lens air-dry completely before replacing caps or filters.

Protecting Lenses from Scratches and Damage

Use Lens Caps

- Always keep lens caps on when not in use to prevent accidental scratches or dust accumulation.

Invest in UV Filters

- Attach a UV filter to protect the front element from physical damage or dirt.
- Example: A UV filter acts as a shield against scratches while preserving image quality.

Avoid Harsh Environments

- Protect your lens from sand, water, or extreme temperatures by using weather-resistant gear.
- Example: Use a rain cover when shooting in wet conditions.

Store Properly

- Keep lenses in padded bags or cases when traveling to prevent impact damage.
- Example: Use dividers in camera bags to avoid lenses rubbing against each other.

Practical Examples of Cleaning Effects

Scenario	Before	After
Fingerprint Smudge	Blurry spot in center of image	Clear, sharp focus
Dust Accumulation	Reduced contrast; hazy appearance	Vibrant colors; crisp details
Water Droplet Residue	Distorted light reflections	Smooth light transmission

Proper cleaning and care are essential for maintaining your camera lenses' performance and longevity. By following safe cleaning practices — using air blowers, microfiber cloths, and gentle cleaning solutions — you can ensure your lenses remain free of smudges and scratches while delivering sharp images every time. Additionally, protecting your lenses with caps, filters, and proper storage will prevent unnecessary wear and tear, allowing you to focus on capturing stunning photos without interruptions!

Conclusion: Your Journey to Photography Mastery

Throughout this comprehensive guide, you've embarked on a transformative journey to master photography with your Samsung Galaxy S25 Ultra. From understanding the basics of composition and lighting to leveraging advanced AI features and troubleshooting common issues, you've gained a wealth of knowledge to elevate your photography skills. This conclusion recaps the key takeaways, encourages continued practice, and provides resources for further learning.

Key Takeaways from Your Journey

1. **Composition Techniques**:

    o   Mastered the rule of thirds, leading lines, and symmetry to create visually appealing compositions.

    o   Learned how to use negative space effectively for minimalist shots.

2. **Lighting and Exposure**:

    o   Understood how to work with natural light, artificial light, and mixed lighting conditions.

- o Adjusted exposure settings for optimal results in various scenarios.

3. **AI Features and Editing**:

   - o Explored AI Scene Optimization, Object Eraser, and Background Blur for enhancing photos.

   - o Learned how to use third-party editing apps like Adobe Lightroom and Snapseed.

4. **Specialized Photography Scenarios**:

   - o Developed skills in travel, food, and social media content creation.

   - o Experimented with low-light and night photography techniques.

5. **Troubleshooting and Maintenance**:

   - o Identified common camera issues and learned troubleshooting techniques.

   - o Mastered storage management and lens care for long-term equipment health.

Next Steps: Continuing Your Photography Journey

1. **Practice Regularly**:

- Continue experimenting with new techniques and styles to refine your skills.

- Set aside time each week to capture new photos and reflect on your progress.

2. **Experiment with New Techniques**:

- Try different genres like street photography or wildlife photography.

- Explore advanced features like RAW shooting and manual focus.

3. **Join Photography Communities**:

- Engage with online forums like Reddit's r/photography or local photography clubs.

- Share your work and learn from others by participating in critiques and discussions.

4. **Pursue Further Learning**:

- Enroll in online courses on platforms like Udemy, Coursera, or Skillshare.

- Follow photography blogs and YouTube channels for tutorials and inspiration.

Recommended Resources for Further Learning

Resource	Description	Benefits
Udemy Courses	Comprehensive courses on photography basics and advanced techniques	Structured learning with expert instructors
Skillshare	Workshops and classes focused on creative photography projects	Hands-on projects and community feedback
Reddit's r/photography	Active community for sharing work, asking questions, and learning from others	Real-time feedback and diverse perspectives
YouTube Channels	Channels like Tony Northrup, Peter McKinnon, and Mango Street Lab	Tutorials, gear reviews, and creative inspiration

Final Thoughts

Your journey to photography mastery is ongoing, and there's always room for growth and exploration. By continuing to practice, experiment with new techniques, and engage with the photography community, you'll refine your skills and develop a unique style that reflects your creativity and passion. Remember, photography is a lifelong journey, and the more you learn, the more you'll discover new ways to express yourself through the lens of your Galaxy S25 Ultra!

www.ingramcontent.com/pod-product-compliance
Lightning Source LLC
LaVergne TN
LVHW051341050326
832903LV00031B/3667